Conquering
An Enemy Called Average

by

John Mason

4th Printing
Over 65,000 in Print

Conquering an Enemy Called Average
ISBN: 1-888103-08-6
Copyright © 1996 by John Mason
Published by Insight International
P. O. Box 54996
Tulsa, Oklahoma 74155

CONTENTS

DEDICATION

It gives me great pleasure to dedicate this book to my wonderful wife Linda and our four great kids: Michelle, Greg, Mike & Dave.

To Linda, thanks for the fun and fullness
you bring to my life;

To Michelle, thanks for the love
you show "dear old dad";

To Greg, thanks for being a fine young man
and my golfing buddy;

To Mike, thanks for your
hilarious inventiveness;

To Dave, thanks for that incredibly
contagious smile.

ACKNOWLEDGEMENTS

I would like to thank four great friends whose words and actions always leave me better than they found me.

To Mike Loomis, for being a contagious
carrier of faith and God's best for me;

To Tim Redmond, for your discernment
and enthusiasm for my life;

To Bill Scheer, for your no-holds-barred
way of living for God;

To Tom Winters, for your consistent
counsel and excellent wisdom.

INTRODUCTION

Recently I spoke at a conference on "How to Get Your Book Published." The first question I was asked was, "Did you always know that you would be a writer?" My answer was, "If , while I was in college, someone had asked me to list fifty things that I thought I would do with my life, writing a book would not have been one of them." I am always amazed each time I write a book at how God can use a person like me to do it.

That is what this book is all about. God has a plan for your life and His plans are good. Some of those plans you may know now and some of them you may not know. My purpose in writing this book is to attack any area in your life that would hold you back from becoming all that you can be.

This book is a special book for me and I believe it will be for you also. This book, *Conquering An Enemy Called Average*, is the sequel to my first book, *An Enemy Called Average*. Although I have now written eight books, there is a special place reserved in my heart for my first one.

As you read this book, expect to be challenged like never before. Trust God to speak to you and direct your steps. Anticipate new ideas and enthusiasm coming into your life. Believe for permanent and enduring changes.

Thank you for the privilege of investing in your life!

John Mason

LOOKING INWARD

NUGGET #1

KNOW YOUR LIMITS,
THEN IGNORE THEM!

L ife is too short to think small. Rather do as my pastor, Joel Budd, encourages us to do, "March off the map." Most people could do more than they think they can, but they usually do less than they think they can. You never know what you cannot do until you try. I agree with Oscar Wilde when he said, "Moderation is a fatal thing. Nothing succeeds like excess." Everything is possible — never use the word never. Charles Schwab said, "When a man has put a limit on what he will do he has put a limit on what he can do."

Dr. J.A. Holmes said, "Never tell a young person that something cannot be done. God may have been waiting for centuries for somebody ignorant enough of the impossible to do that thing." If *you* devalue your dreams, rest assured the world won't raise the price. You will find that great leaders are rarely "realistic" by other people's standards.

The answer to your future lies outside the confines that you have right now. If you want to see if you can really swim, don't frustrate yourself with shallow water. Cavett Robert said, "Any man who selects a goal in life which can be fully achieved has already defined his own limitations." Rather be as Art Sepulveda said, "Be a history maker and a world shaker." Go where you have never gone before.

Ronald McNair says, "You only become a winner if you are willing to walk over the edge." Capture Randy Loescher's perspective: "God says, 'Ask me for the mountain'." The Bible says, "Things which are impossible with men are possible with God" (Luke 18:27). Take the lid off.

When you climb the tallest tree, you win the right to the best fruit. Dag Hammarskjold said, "Is life so wretched? Is it rather your hands which are too small, your vision which is muddled? You are the one who must grow up." Gloria Swanson said, "Never say never. Never is a long, undependable thing, and life is too full of rich possibilities to have restrictions placed upon it."

To believe an idea impossible is to make it so. Consider how many fantastic projects have miscarried because of small thinking or have been strangled in their birth by a cowardly imagination. I like what Marabeau said. When he heard the word "impossible," he responded, "Never let me hear that foolish word again."

Pearl Buck said, "All things are possible until they are proved impossible — even the impossible may only be so as of now." John Ruskin said, "Dream lofty dreams and as you dream, so you shall become. Your vision is the promise of what you shall at last unveil." Somebody is always doing what somebody else said couldn't be done. Dare to think unthinkable thoughts.

Develop an infinite capacity to ignore what others think can't be done. Don't just grow where you are planted. Bloom where you are planted and bear fruit. Daniel Webster said, "There is always room at the top." No one can predict to what heights you can soar. Even you will not know until you spread your wings.

NONE OF THE SECRETS OF SUCCESS
WILL WORK UNLESS YOU DO.

You can't fulfill your destiny on a theory... it takes WORK. You are made for action. It is much more natural for you to be doing than sitting. Success simply takes good ideas and puts them into action. What the *free enterprise* system really means is that the more *enterprising* you are the more *free* you are. What this country needs is less emphasis on *free* and more on *enterprise*.

Listen to Shakespeare: "Nothing can come of nothing." A belief is worthless unless converted into action. The word *work* is not an obscure biblical concept; it appears in the Bible over 500 times. Often, the simple answer to your prayer is: *Go to work*.

"Striving for success without hard work is like trying to harvest where you haven't planted" (David Bly). What you believe doesn't amount to very much unless it causes you to climb out of the grandstand and onto the playing field. You cannot just dream yourself into what you could be. The only time a lazy person ever succeeds is when he tries to do nothing. A famous old saying says it best: "Laziness travels so slowly, poverty soon overtakes it."

A person who wastes enormous amounts of time talking about success will win the "prize" of failure. When you are lazy, you must work twice. It is always a trying time for the person who is always trying to get something for nothing. God doesn't make apple juice — He makes apples. Some say *nothing* is impossible, yet there are a lot of people doing *nothing* every day.

Some do things while others sit around becoming experts on how things might be done. The world is divided into people who do things and people who talk about doing things. Belong to the first group — there is far less competition.

I believe the Lord didn't burden us with work. He blessed us with it. "All men are alike in their promises. It is only in their deeds that they differ" (Moliere). Wishing has never made a poor man wealthy. Robert Half nails it: "Laziness is the secret ingredient that goes into failure, but it's only kept a secret from the person who fails."

Tell yourself: "Inspirations never go in for long engagements; they demand immediate marriage to action" (Brendon Francis). If the truth were known, most of our troubles arise from loafing when we should be working, and talking when we should be listening.

> There is a man in the world who never gets turned down, wherever he chances to stray;
> he gets the glad hand in the populous town, or out where the farmers make hay;
> he is greeted with pleasure on deserts of sand, and deep in the isles of the woods;
> wherever he goes there is a welcoming hand —
> he's the man who delivers the goods.
>
> Walt Whitman

THERE'S NOTHING IN THE MIDDLE OF THE ROAD BUT YELLOW STRIPES AND DEAD ARMADILLOS.

— James Hightower

"My decision is maybe — and that's final." Is this you? Being decisive is essential for a successful life. If you deny yourself commitment, what will you do with your life? Every accomplishment, great or small, starts with a decision.

Choice, not chance, determines destiny. Too many people go through life not knowing what they want, but feeling sure they don't have it. Herbert Prochnow said, "There is a time when we must firmly choose the course which we will follow, or the relentless drift of events will make the decision for us."

Too many people are like wheelbarrows, trailers, or canoes. They need to be pushed, pulled or paddled. You're either moving other people to decisions or they're moving you. Decide to do something now to make *your* life better. The choice is yours.

David Ambrose remarked, "If you have the will to win, you have achieved half your success; if you don't, you have achieved half your failure." Lou Holtz said, "If you don't make a total commitment to whatever you are doing then you start looking to bail out the first time the boat starts leaking. It's tough enough getting the boat to shore with everybody rowing, let alone when a guy stands up and starts putting his life jacket on."

The moment you definitely commit yourself, God moves too. All sorts of things happen to help you that never would have otherwise occurred. Edgar Roberts said, "Every human mind is a great slumbering power until awakened by a keen desire and a definite resolution to do." Kenneth Blanchard observed, "There is a difference between interests and commitment. When you are interested in doing something, you only do it when it is convenient. When you are committed to something, you accept no excuses, only results." Lack of decisiveness has caused more failures than lack of intelligence or ability.

Maurice Witzer said, "You seldom get what you go after unless you know in advance what you want." Indecision often gives an advantage to the other person because they did their thinking beforehand. Helen Keller said, "Science may have found a cure for most evil; but it has found no remedy for the worst of them all — the apathy of human beings." Joshua encourages, "Choose for yourselves this day whom you will serve..." (Joshua 24:15). Don't leave a decision for tomorrow that needs to be made today.

Bertrand Russel said, "Nothing is so exhausting as indecision, and nothing is so futile." Joseph Newton discerned, "Not what we have, but what we use, not what we see, but what we choose — these are things that mar or bless human happiness." Remember, don't be a "middle-of-the-roader" because the middle of the road is the worst place to try to go forward. Today, decide on your dream.

NUGGET #4

YOU CAN'T TRAVEL THE ROAD TO SUCCESS WITHOUT A PUNCTURE OR TWO.

Paul Galvin at the age of thirty-three had failed twice in business. He attended an auction of his own storage battery business. With his last $750, he bought back the battery eliminator portion of it. That part became Motorola. Upon his retirement in the 1960's, he said, "Do not fear mistakes. You will know failure. Continue to reach out." George Bernard Shaw said, "A life spent making mistakes is more useful than a life spent doing nothing." To expect life to be perfectly tailored to our specifications is to live a life of continual frustration. When you make mistakes, just learn from them and don't respond with encores.

David McNally mused, "The mistake riddled life is much richer, more interesting, and more stimulating than the life that has never risked or taken a stand on anything." What is the difference between champions and the average person? Tom Hopkins says, "The single most important difference between champion achievers and average people is their ability to handle rejection and failure." Listen to S. I. Hayakawa: "Notice the difference between what happens when a man says to himself, 'I failed three times,' and what happens when he says, 'I am a failure'." Failure is a situation, never a person.

Mistakes are often the best teachers. The Bible says in Ecclesiastes, "In the day of prosperity be joyful, but in the day of adversity consider" (7:14). Oswald Avery advises, "Whenever you fall, pick something up." The man who invented the eraser had the human race pretty well sized up. You will find that people who never make mistakes never make anything else. It's true: you can profit from your mistakes. That's why I am convinced I'll be a millionaire.

Failure is not falling down, but staying down. Be like Jonah, who proved that you can't keep a good man down. Remember a stumble is not a fall. In fact, a stumble may prevent a fall. Proverbs reads, "For though a righteous man falls seven times, he rises again" (24:16 NIV). Herman Melville wrote, "He who has never failed somewhere, that man cannot be great."

The person who never makes a mistake takes orders from and lives his life for someone who does. William Ward said, "Failure is delay, but not defeat. It is a temporary detour, not a dead end street." Not remembered for his failures but for his successes, inventor Thomas Edison reflected, "People are not remembered by how few times they failed, but by how often they succeed." Every wrong step can be another step forward. David Burns said, "Assert your right to make a few mistakes. If people can't accept your imperfection, that's their fault."

Louis Boone said, "Don't fear failure so much that you refuse to try new things. The saddest summary of life contains three descriptions, could have, might have, and should have." Robert Schuller wrote, "Look at what you have left, never look at what you have lost." If you learn from them, mistakes are useful. Cultivate this attitude and you will never be ashamed to try. Uncover the jewels from your mistakes.

IMITATION IS LIMITATION.

"If God had wanted you otherwise, He would have created you otherwise" (Goethe). Dare to be what you are. Resolve to be yourself. A Congolese proverb asserts, "Wood may remain ten years in the water, but it will never become a crocodile." The Bible asks, "Can the Ethiopian change his skin or the leopard his spots?" (Jeremiah 13:23) Julius Hare advises, "Be what you are. This is the first step towards becoming better than you are."

"My mother said to me, 'If you become a soldier you'll become a general, if you become a monk you'll end up as the pope.' Instead, I became a painter and wound up as Picasso," said the great painter. No one ever became great by imitation. Don't be a copy of something. Make your own impression.

"The curious paradox is that when I accept myself just as I am, then I can change" (Carl Rogers). Worn out paths are for worn out men. Friedrich Klopstock remarked, "He who has no opinion of his own, but depends on the opinions of others is a slave. To only dream of the person you are supposed to be is to waste the person you are." Nobody is so disappointed and so unhappy as the person who longs all of life to be somebody other than who he really is.

The person who trims himself to suit everybody will soon whittle himself away. All people are created equal and endowed by their Creator with a mighty urge to become otherwise. If you don't have a plan for your own life, you'll only become a part of someone else's. You can't carry two faces under one hat. Never wish to be anything but what you are. "It is better to be hated for what you are, than loved for what you are not" (Andre Gide).

"All the discontented people I know are trying to be something they are not, to do something they cannot do" (David Grayson). When you will not dare to be yourself, you will lack confidence and will crave admiration continually. You will live on the reflection of yourself in the eyes of others.

"Man is more interesting than men. It's him, not them, whom God made in his image. Each is more precious than all" (Andre Gide). "All good things which exist are the fruit of originality" (John Mills). There is only one life for each of us — our own. The person who walks in another's tracks never leaves his own footprints. Doris Mortman observed, "Until you make peace with who you are, you will never be content with what you have." Most of our challenges in life come from not knowing ourselves and ignoring our best, real virtues.

Most people live their entire lives as complete strangers to themselves. Don't let that happen to you. The Bible says in 1 Kings, "Why feignest thou thyself to be another?" (14:5) Leo Buscaglia counseled, "The easiest thing to be in the world is you. The most difficult thing to be is what other people want you to be. Don't let them put you in that position." The opposite of courage is not fear. It is conformity. The most exhausting and frustrating thing in life is to live it trying to be someone else.

24

NUGGET #6

SAFETY LAST!

For many years " 'Safety first' has been the motto of the human race… but it has never been the motto of leaders. A leader must face danger. He must take the risk and the blame and the brunt of the storm" (Herbert Casson). If you want to be successful, you must either have a chance or take one. You can't get your head above water if you never stick your neck out.

A dream that does not include risk is not really worthy of being called a dream. Halifax said, "The man who leaves nothing to chance will do few things badly, but he will do very few things." If you'll never take risks, you'll never accomplish great things. Everybody dies, but not everyone has lived.

C. S. Lewis said, "The safest road to hell is a gradual one — the gentle slope, soft under foot, without sudden turnings, without milestones, without sign posts." Elizabeth Kenny reflected, "It is better to be a lion for a day than a sheep all your life." If you dare for nothing, you need hope for nothing.

If you don't risk anything you risk even more. John Newman wrote, "Calculation never made a hero." Every person has a chance to improve himself, but some just don't believe in taking chances. I agree with Lois Platford when she said, "You have all eternity to be cautious and then you're dead." Being destined for greatness requires you to take risks and confront great hazards.

You'll always miss 100% of the shots that you don't take. I agree with Stemmons when he said, "When your chances are slim and none... go with slim." Morris West said, "If you spend your whole life inside waiting for the storms, you'll never enjoy the sunshine." No one reaches the top without daring.

Listen to Conrad Hilton: "I encourage boldness because the danger of seniority and pension plans tempt a young man to settle in a rut named security rather than find his own rainbow." Chuck Yeager remarked, "You don't concentrate on risk. You concentrate on results. No risk is too great to prevent the necessary job from getting done."

Whenever you see a successful person, I guarantee that person took risks and made courageous decisions. Success favors the bold. The world is a book where those who do not take risks read only one page. David Mahoney said, "Refuse to join the cautious crowd that plays not to lose. Play to win."

Metastaisio observed, "Every noble acquisition is attended with its risk; he who fears to encounter the one must not expect to obtain the other." Listen to Tommy Barnett: "Many people believe that you are really walking by faith when there is no risk but the truth is the longer you walk with God... the greater the risk." If you have found yourself throughout life never scared, embarrassed, disappointed or hurt it means you have never taken any chances.

David Viscot wrote, "If your life is ever going to get better, you'll have to take risks. There is simply no way you can grow without taking chances." You have a chance to improve yourself. Just believe in taking chances.

DO MORE...

Do more than exist, live.

Do more than hear, listen.

Do more than agree, cooperate.

Do more than talk, communicate.

Do more than grow, bloom.

Do more than spend, invest.

Do more than think, create.

Do more than work, excel.

Do more than share, give.

Do more than decide, discern.

Do more than consider, commit.

Do more than forgive, forget.

Do more than help, serve.

Do more than coexist, reconcile.

Do more than sing, worship.

Do more than think, plan.

Do more than dream, do.

Do more than see, perceive.

Do more than read, apply.

Do more than receive, reciprocate.

Do more than choose, focus.

Do more than wish, believe.

Do more than advise, help.

Do more than speak, impart.

Do more than encourage, inspire.

Do more than add, multiply.

Do more than change, improve.

Do more than reach, stretch.

Do more than ponder, pray.

NUGGET #8

THE ONLY PLACE TO START IS WHERE YOU ARE.

Start with what you have, not with what you don't have. Opportunity is always where you are, never where you were. To get anywhere you must launch out for somewhere or you will get nowhere. Hamilton Mabie said, "The question for each man to settle is not what he would do if he had the means, time, influence and education advantages, but what he will do with the things he has." God will always give us an ability to create what we need from something that is already here.

Each person tends to underrate or overrate that which they do not possess. Ed Howe said, "People are always neglecting something they can do and trying to do something they can't do." I agree with Teddy Roosevelt when he said, "Do what you can, with what you have, where you are." The only way to learn anything thoroughly is by starting at the bottom (except when learning how to swim). To be successful, do what you can.

Ken Keys, Jr. said, "To be upset over what you don't have is to waste what you do have." The truth is that many are successful because they didn't have the advantages others had. People with enterprise accomplish more than others because they go ahead and do it before they are ready.

Epicurus said, "Do not spoil what you have by desiring what you have not; but remember that what you now have was once among the things only hoped for." Henri Amiel observed, "Almost everything comes from almost nothing."

No improvement is so certain as that which proceeds from the right and timely use of what you already have. Mike Murdock said, "Whatever God has already given to you will create anything else He has promised to you." Everyone who has arrived had to begin where they were.

The truth is, you can't know what you can do until you try. The most important thing about reaching your dream is starting right where you are. Edward Hail said, "I cannot do everything, but I still can do something; and because I cannot do everything, I will not refuse to do something I can do."

> No longer forward nor behind
> I look in hope or fear;
> but, grateful, take the good I find,
> the best of now and here.

John Greenleaf Whittier

30

NOAH DIDN'T WAIT FOR HIS SHIP TO COME IN — HE BUILT ONE.

Seize the moment! "Miracles are coming by you or to you every day" (Oral Roberts). Today was once the future from which you expected so much in the past. Horatio Dresser said, "The ideal never comes. Today is ideal for him who makes it so." Live for today. Don't let what you have within your grasp today be missed entirely because only the future intrigued you and the past disheartened you.

Doing the best at this moment puts you in the best place for the next moment. When can you live if not now? All the flowers of tomorrow are in the seeds of today. Seneca said, "Begin at once to live." Ellen Metcalf remarked, "There are many people who are at the right place at the right time but don't know it." It is okay to take time to plan, but when the time of action has arrived, stop thinking and go for it!

The Bible says, "Lord, teach us to number our days, that we may apply our hearts unto wisdom" (Ps 90:12). Marie Edgeworth said, "There is no moment like the present. The man who will not execute his resolutions when they are fresh on him can have no hope from them afterwards; for they will be dissipated, lost, and perished in the hurry and scurry of the world, or sunk in the slough of indolence."

John Burroughs said, "The lesson which life repeats and constantly reinforces is, 'Look under foot.' You are always nearer than you think. The great opportunity is where you are. Do not despise your own place and hour." The most important thing in our lives is what we are doing now.

Know the real value of today. I agree with Jonathan Swift when he said, "May you live all the days of your life." The future that you long and dream for begins today. Ralph Waldo Emerson said, "Write it on your heart that every day is the best day of the year."

The regrets that most people experience in life come from failing to act when having an opportunity. Albert Dunning said, "Great opportunities come to all, but many do not know that they have met them. The only preparation to take advantage of them is… to watch what each day brings." Heed 2 Corinthians 6:2: "Now is the accepted time." I agree with Martial when he said, "Tomorrow life is too late; live today." Wayne Dyer observed, "Now is all we have. Everything that has ever happened, anything that is ever going to happen to you, is just a thought." Today, well lived, will prepare you for both the opportunities and obstacles of tomorrow.

Few know when to rise to the occasion. Most only know when to sit down. Many spend too much time dreaming of the future, never realizing that a little of it arrives every day. I agree with Ruth Schabacker when she said, "Every day comes bearing its own gifts. Untie the ribbons."

NUGGET #10

LIVING A DOUBLE LIFE WILL GET YOU NOWHERE TWICE AS FAST.

Character is something you either have or are. Some people try to make something for themselves. Others try to make something of themselves. Tryon Edwards said, "Thoughts lead on to purposes; purposes go forth in action; actions form habits; habits decide character; and character fixes our destiny." The Bible asserts in Proverbs 22:1, "A good name is rather to be chosen than great riches."

Character is the real foundation of all worthwhile success. A good question to ask yourself is, "What kind of world would this world be if everybody were just like you?" You are simply a book telling the world about its author. John Morely remarked, "No man can climb out beyond the limitations of his own character."

Never be ashamed of doing right. Marcus Aurelius exhorted, "Never esteem as of advantage to thee that which shall make thee break thy word or lose thy self-respect." W. J. Dawson counseled, "You need not choose evil; but only to fail to choose good, and you drift fast enough towards evil. You do not need to say, 'I will be bad,' you only have to say, 'I will not choose God's choice,' and the choice of evil is already settled." There is no such thing as a *necessary evil*. Phillip Brooks said, "A man who lives right and is right has more power in his silence than another has by his words."

33

Many a man's reputation would not recognize his character if they met in the dark. To change your character, you must begin at the control center — the heart. Spiritual bankruptcy is inevitable when a man is no longer able to keep the interest paid on his moral obligations.

Henry Ward Beecher said, "No man can tell whether he is rich or poor by turning to his ledger. It is the heart that makes a man rich. He is rich according to what he is, not according to what he has." Live so that your friends can defend you, but never have to do so. Consider what Woodrow Wilson said: "If you think about what you ought to do for people, your character will take care of itself." Excellence in character is shown by doing unwitnessed what we would be doing with the whole world watching.

Let me pose this question for you: *Would the boy you were be proud of the man you are?* You're called to grow like a tree, not like a mushroom. It's hard to climb high when your character is low. The world's shortest sermon is preached by the traffic sign: *Keep Right.*

NUGGET #11

THE MOST UNPROFITABLE ITEM EVER MANUFACTURED IS AN EXCUSE.

When it comes to excuses, the world is full of great inventors. Some spend half their lives telling what they are going to do, and the other half explaining why they didn't do it. An alibi is the proof that you did do what you didn't do, so that others will think you didn't do what you did.

You can fail many times but not be a failure until you begin to blame someone else. Our own mistakes fail in their mission of helping us when we blame them on other people. When you use excuses you give up your power to change.

You treat others right when you don't blame them for anything that is really wrong with you. "Never mind whom you praise, but be careful whom you blame" (Edmond Gosse). You can fall down many times, but you won't be a failure until you say that someone else pushed you.

If you can find an excuse, don't use it. Most failures are experts at making excuses. There are always enough excuses available if you are weak enough to use them. The world simply does not have enough crutches for all the lame excuses. It's always easier to find excuses instead of time for the things we don't want to do.

So, find a way, not an excuse. There is no excuse for a human being full of excuses. One who makes a mistake, and then makes an excuse for it, is making two mistakes. Note this truth: "The fox condemns the trap, not himself" (Blake). Don't find yourself talking like that old fox!

Never complain and never explain. "Admitting errors clears the score and proves you wiser than before" (Arthur Guiterman). Doing a job right is always easier than fabricating an alibi for why you didn't. The devil eagerly waits to provide you with an excuse for every sin. Time wasted thinking up excuses and alibis would always be better spent praying, planning, preparing and working towards your goals in life.

NUGGET #12

TODAY A READER, TOMORROW A LEADER.

— W. FUSSELMAN

Have you ever noticed there are people you know who are literally at the same place today as they were five years ago? They still have the same dreams, the same problems, the same alibis, the same opportunities and the same way of thinking. They are standing still in life.

Many people literally unplug their clocks at a certain point in time and stay at that fixed moment the rest of their lives. God's will for us is to grow, to continue to learn and improve. The biggest room in our house is always the room for self-improvement.

A famous saying reads: "It's what you learn after you know it all that counts." I must admit that I am somewhat of a fanatic about this. I hate to have idle time — time in which I am not learning anything. Those around me know that I must always have something to read or to write during any idle moment that might arise. In fact, I try to learn from everyone. From one I may learn what not to do, while from another, I learn what to do. Learn from the mistakes of others. You can never live long enough to make all the mistakes yourself. You can learn more from a wise man when he is wrong than a fool who is right.

Goethe said, "Everybody wants to be: nobody wants to grow." I agree with Van Crouch: "You will never change your actions until you change your mind." An important way to keep growing is to never stop asking questions. The person who is afraid of asking is ashamed of learning. Only hungry minds can grow. We should all know what we are running from and to and why.

We should learn as if we will live forever and live as if we are going to die tomorrow. Harvey Ullman said, "Anyone who stops learning is old, whether this happens at 20 or 80. Anyone who keeps on learning not only remains young, but becomes consistently more valuable regardless of physical capacity." Timothy is instructed: "Study to show thyself approved unto God...." (2 Timothy 2:15). It's fun to keep learning. Learning brings approval to your life.

Learn from others. Learn to see in the challenges of others, the ills you should avoid. Experience is a present possession that keeps us from repeating the past in the future. Life teaches us by giving us new problems before we solve the old ones. Think education is expensive or difficult? Listen to Derek Bok: "If you think education is expensive — try ignorance."

NUGGET #13

STATUS QUO.
(LATIN FOR "THE MESS WE'RE IN.")

Change. I hope this word doesn't scare you, but rather, inspires you. Herbert Spencer said, "A living thing is distinguished from a dead thing by the multiplicity of the changes at any moment taking place in it." Change is an evidence of life. It is impossible to grow without change. Those who cannot change their minds cannot change anything. The truth is, life is always at some turning point.

What people want is progress, if they can have it without change. Impossible! You must change and recognize that change is your greatest ally. The person who never changes his opinion, never corrects his mistakes. The fact is, the road to success is always under construction.

Yesterday's formula for success is often tomorrow's recipe for failure. Consider what Thomas Watson, the founder of the IBM Corporation, said, "There is a world market for about 5 computers." Where would IBM be today if Mr. Watson had not been willing to change?

You cannot become what you are destined to be by remaining what you are. John Patterson said, "Only fools and dead men don't change their minds. Fools won't. Dead men can't." If you don't respect the need for change consider this: How many things have you seen that have changed just in the past year? When you change yourself, opportunities will change. The same kind of thinking that has brought you to where you are, will not necessarily get you to where you want to go. Sante Boeve discovered this truth: "There are people whose watch stops at a certain hour and who remain permanently at that age."

Do not fear change, for it is an unchangeable law of progress. The man who uses yesterday's methods in today's world won't be in business tomorrow. A traditionalist is simply a person whose mind is always open to new ideas, provided they are the same old ones. "There are people who not only strive to remain static themselves, but strive to keep everything else so... their position is almost laughably hopeless" (Odell Shepard).

Mignon McLaughlin said, "It's the most unhappy people who most fear change." When patterns and tradition are broken, new opportunities come together. Defending your faults and errors only proves that you have no intention of quitting them. All progress is due to those who were not satisfied to let well enough alone. They weren't afraid to change. Change is not your enemy — it is your friend.

GET AHEAD OF YOURSELF.

"**O**ur business in life is not to get ahead of others, but to get ahead of ourselves — to break our own records, to outstrip our yesterdays by today, to do our work with more force than ever before" (Stewart Johnson). If you would like to know who is responsible for most of your troubles, take a look in the mirror. If you could kick the fellow responsible for most of your problems, you wouldn't be able to sit down for three weeks. It's time for us to stay out of our own way.

Most of the stumbling blocks people complain about are under their own hats. Louis XIV commented, "There is little that can withstand a man who can conquer himself." The Bible's wisdom counsels, "He that hath no rule over his own spirit is like a city that is broken down, and without walls" (Proverbs 25:28).

"Your future depends on many things, but mostly on you" (Frank Tyger). You may succeed if nobody else believes in you, but you will never succeed if you don't believe in yourself. Zig Ziglar observes, "What you picture in your mind, your mind will go to work to accomplish. When you change your pictures you automatically change your performance." Whatever you attach consistently to the words "I am", you will become.

Ralph Waldo Emerson said, "It is impossible for man to be cheated by anyone but himself." Gain control of your mind or it will gain control of you. Your imagination dictates your openness to positive direction. As Norman Vincent Peale remarked, "Do not build up obstacles in your imagination. Remind yourself that God is with you and that nothing can defeat Him."

"Our best friends and our worst enemies are the thoughts we have about ourselves" (Dr. Frank Crane). Stop looking only at where you are and start looking at what you can be. The Bible declares, "As a man thinketh, so is he, and as a man chooseth so is he" (Proverbs 23:7). Be careful of your thoughts. They may become words at any moment and actions very soon. Wrong thinking almost always leads to misery.

No one can defeat you unless you first defeat yourself. Self-image sets the boundaries and limits of each of our individual accomplishments. Charles Colton said, "We are sure to be losers when we quarrel with ourselves; it is civil war." If you doubt yourself, listen to Alexander Dumas: "A person who doubts himself is like a man who enlists in the ranks of his enemy and bears arms against himself." Tim Redmond observed, "Don't commit treason against your own life and purpose."

Your world first exists within you. Marriane Crawford said, "Every man carries with him the world in which he must live." Having trouble hearing from God? "When God speaks, your mind will be your biggest enemy" (Bob Harrison). Facing major obstacles in life? James Allen answered, "You are the handicap you must face. You are the one who must choose your place." Remember you are your own doctor when it comes to curing cold feet, a hot head and a stuffy attitude.

TO FINISH FIRST
YOU MUST FIRST FINISH.
— RICK MEARS

Do you want to accomplish something in life? Be like the stone cutter. Jacob Riis says, "Look at the stone cutter hammering away at the rock, perhaps a 100 times without as much as a crack showing in it. Yet at the 101st blow it will split in two and I know it was not the last blow that did it, but all that had gone before." Whatever you want to accomplish in life will require persistence.

All things come to those who go after them. Perseverance is the result of a strong will. Stubbornness is the result of a strong won't. Montesquieu said, "Success often depends on knowing how long it will take to succeed." The secret of success: never let down and never let up. Many times success consists of hanging on one minute longer.

Calvin Coolidge said, " 'Press on' has solved and always will solve the problems of the human race." James 5:11 reads, "Behold we count them happy which endure." You will find that persistent people always have this attitude: they never lose the game, they just run out of time. All spiritual progress is like an unfolding vegetable bud. You first have a leading, then peace, then conviction, as the plant has root, bud and fruit. Compte de Buffon says, "Never think that God's delays are God's denials. Hold on; hold fast; hold out. Patience is genius."

43

Joel Hause said, "You may be whatever you resolve to be. Determine to be something in the world and you will be something. 'I cannot' never accomplished anything; 'I will try' has wrought wonders." Herbert Caufman adds, "Spurts don't count. The final score makes no mention of a splendid start if the finish proves that you were 'an also ran'." Keep in mind the words of Hamilton Holt: "Nothing worthwhile comes easily. Half effort does not produce half results. It produces no results. Work, continuous work and hard work is the only way to accomplish results that last."

Persistence prevails when all else fails. Revelations 2:10 says, "Be faithful unto death, and I will give thee a crown of life." The truth is that persistence is a bitter plant, but it has sweet fruit. Joseph Ross said, "It takes time to succeed because success is merely the natural reward of taking time to do anything well." Ecclesiastes declares, "Better is the end of a thing than the beginning thereof; and the patient in spirit is better than the proud in spirit" (7:8). Victory always comes to the most persevering.

Ralph Waldo Emerson said, "The great majority of men are bundles of beginnings." I agree with Charles Kettering when he said, "Keep on going and the chances are you will stumble on something perhaps when you are least expecting it." No one finds life worth living. One must make it worth living. Persistence is the quality that is most needed when it is exhausted. Often genius is just another way of spelling persistence.

NUGGET #16

WHITE LIES LEAVE BLACK MARKS.

There is no limit to the height a man can attain by remaining on the level. Honesty is still the best policy. However, today there are less policy holders than there used to be. George Braque said, "Truth exists, only falsehood has to be invented." Cervantes said, "Truth will rise above falsehood as oil above water."

White lies leave black marks on a man's reputation. You can't stretch the truth without making your story look pretty thin. When you stretch the truth, it will snap back at you. Truth will win every argument if you stick with it long enough. Though truth may not be popular, it is always right. The fact that nobody wants to believe something, doesn't keep it from being true.

Two half-truths do not necessarily constitute the whole truth. In fact, beware of half-truths. You may have gotten hold of the wrong half. You will find that a lie has no legs. It has to be supported by other lies. The truth is one thing for which there are no known substitutes. There is no acceptable substitute for honesty. There is no valid excuse for dishonesty.

Nothing shows dirt like a white lie. At times a fib starts out as a little white lie, but it usually ends up as a double feature in technicolor. It may appear to you that a lie may take care of the present, but I want to let you know it has no future.

The only way to truly be free is to be a person of truth. John 8:32 asserts, "And you shall know the truth and the truth shall make you free." Truth is strong and it will prevail.

A shady person never produces a bright life. Herbert Casson said, "Show me a liar and I will show you a thief." A liar will not be believed even though he tells the truth. George Bernard Shaw said, "The liar's punishment is not in the least that he is not believed, but that he cannot believe anyone else."

Liars have no true friends. "If you lie and then tell the truth, the truth will be considered a lie" (Sumerian). An honest man alters his ideas to fit the truth and a dishonest man alters the truth to fit his ideas. There are no degrees of honesty.

The Bible says, "Let not mercy and truth forsake thee; bind them about thy neck; write them upon the tablet of thine heart" (Proverbs 3:3). M. Runbeck said, "There is no power on earth more formidable than the truth." Consider what Pearl Buck said, "Truth is always exciting." Speak it, then. Life is dull without it.

NUGGET #17

THE WORLD BELONGS TO THE ENTHUSIASTIC.

"Think excitement, talk excitement, act out excitement, and you are bound to become an excited person. Life will take on a new zest, deeper interests and greater meaning. You can talk, think, and act yourself into dullness and into monotony or into unhappiness. By the same process you can build up inspiration, excitement and a surging depth of joy" (Norman Vincent Peale). You can succeed at almost anything for which you have limitless enthusiasm. Enthusiasm moves the world.

Your enthusiasm reflects your reserves, your unexploited resources and perhaps your future. One real difference between people is their level of enthusiasm. Winston Churchill said, "Success is going from failure to failure without loss of enthusiasm." You will never rise to great truths and heights without joy and enthusiasm. The Bible says in 2 Chronicles 31:21, "He did it with all his heart and prospered."

"No one keeps up his enthusiasm automatically" (Papyrus). Enthusiasm must be nourished with new actions, new aspirations, new efforts and new vision. It's your own fault if your enthusiasm is gone. You have failed to feed it. What's enthusiasm? Henry Chester answers: "Enthusiasm is nothing more or less than faith in action." Helen Keller said, "Optimism is the faith that leads to achievement." Nothing can be done without hope or confidence.

It isn't our position, but our disposition that makes us happy. Remember, some people freeze in the winter. Others ski. A positive attitude always creates positive results. Attitude is a little thing that makes a big difference. Depression, gloom, pessimism, despair, discouragement and fear slay more human beings than all illnesses combined.

You can't deliver the goods if your heart is heavier than the load. "We act as though comfort and luxury were the chief requirements of life, when all that we need to make us really happy is something to be enthusiastic about" (Charles Kingsley). Some people count their blessings but most think their blessings don't count.

There is a direct correlation between our passion and our potential. Enthusiasm shows God in us. You can be the light of the world, but the switch must be turned on. Being positive is essential to achievement and the foundation of true progress. If you live a life of negativity you will find yourself seasick during the entire voyage. The person who is negative is half-defeated before even beginning.

I agree with Winston Churchill when he said, "I am an optimist. It does not seem too much use being anything else." Have you ever noticed that no matter how many worries a pessimist has, he always has room for one more? Remember the Chinese proverb: "It is better to light a candle than to curse the darkness." Das Energi said, "Vote with your life. Vote yes!"

NUGGET #18

IF YOU CHASE TWO RABBITS, BOTH WILL ESCAPE.

Ask yourself this question, "What am I really aiming at?" Delegate, simplify or eliminate low priorities as soon as possible. Do *more* by doing *less*. James Liter said, "One thought driven home is better than three left on base."

There are too many people in too many cars, in too much of a hurry, going too many directions, to get nowhere for nothing. "There is so little time for the discovery of all that we want to know about things that really interest us. We cannot afford to waste it on things that are only of casual concern for us, or in which we are interested only because other people have told us what we ought to be" (Alec Waugh). For the person who has no focus, there is no peace.

Tim Redmond said, "Don't be a jack of all trades and a master of none. Instead be like the Apostle Paul who wrote, 'This one thing I do...' 'I press towards the mark'" (Philippians 3:14). What you set your heart on will determine how you will spend your life. Carl Sandberg said, "There are people who want to be everywhere at once and they get nowhere."

How can you get what you want? William Locke answered, "I can tell how to get what you want; you just got to keep a thing in view and go for it, and never let your eyes wander to the right or left or up or down. And looking back is fatal." Jesus warns, "No man can serve two masters; for he will either hate the one and love the other; or else he will hold to the one and despise the other" (Matthew 5:24). When you serve two masters, you have to lie to one.

George Bernard Shaw wrote, "Give a man health and a course to steer, and he will never stop to trouble about whether he is happy or not." We know that Walt Disney was successful. Maybe the key to his success is found in his confession: "I love Mickey Mouse more than any women I've ever known." Now, that's focus!

Vic Braden said, "Losers have tons of variety. Champions take pride in just learning to hit the same old boring winners." Consider what George Robson said after winning the Indianapolis 500: "All I had to do was keep turning left."

I believe you will only find happiness when you are in a position of going somewhere wholeheartedly, in one direction without regret or reservation. Do what you are doing while you are doing it. The more complicated you are, the more ineffective you will become.

Mark Twain said, "Behold the fool saith 'Put not all thine eggs in one basket' — which is but a manner of saying, 'Scatter your money and your attention.' But the wise man saith, 'Put all your eggs in one basket and — watch that basket'." The quickest way to do many things is to do only one thing at a time. The only ones who will be remembered are those who have done one thing superbly well. Don't be like the man who said, "I'm focused, it's just on something else."

HAVE THE COURAGE TO LIVE.
ANYONE CAN QUIT.

"The world will always give you the opportunity to quit, but only the world would call quitting an opportunity" (Clint Brown). In trying times, too many people quit trying. One of the most powerful success principles ever preached is: *Never give up!*

As an author, I have the privilege of signing many books. I like to write encouraging expressions in each book before I sign my name. One of my most common encouragements is: *Never give up!* Joel Budd remarked, "It isn't the final say so, unless *you* say so." Richard Nixon mused, "A man is not finished when he is defeated. He is finished when he quits."

Nobody and nothing can keep you down unless you decide not to rise again. H.E. Jansen said, "The man who wins may have been counted out several times, but he didn't hear the referee." Find a way *to*, not a way *not to*. A lazy man is always judged by what he doesn't do. The choice of giving up or going on is a defining moment in your life. You cannot turn back the clock. But you can wind it up again.

Recently, I had the privilege of meeting Peter Lowe, the founder of the very successful, *Success Seminars*. As we talked, he commented, "The most common trait I have found in all people that are successful is that they have conquered the temptation to give up." One of the best ways to give your best a chance is to rise up when you're knocked down.

Too many people stop faster than they start. Instead of stopping, follow this English proverb: "Don't fall before you are pushed." Margaret Thatcher understood the principle of not quitting when she advised, "You may have to fight a battle more than once to win it." David Zucker added, "Quit now, you'll never make it. If you disregard this advice you'll be halfway there."

"I can't!" is the conclusion of fools. Listen to Clare Booth Luce: "There are no hopeless situations, there are only men who have grown hopeless about them." Admiral Chester Nimitz remarked, "God grant me the courage not to give up what I think is right even though I think it is hopeless." Giving up is the ultimate tragedy. The famous boxer, Archie Moore, reflected, "If I don't get off the mat, I'll lose the fight."

The choice is simple. You can either stand up and be counted, or lie down and be counted out. Defeat never comes to people until they admit it. Your success will be measured by your willingness to keep on trying.

NUGGET #20

HE WHO LAUGHS, LASTS.
— R. FULGRAM

There is a facelift you can perform yourself that is guaranteed to improve your appearance. It is called a smile. Laughter is like changing a baby's diaper — it doesn't permanently solve any problems, but it makes things more acceptable for awhile. Cheer up. A dentist is the only person who is supposed to look down in the mouth. Robert Frost says, "Happiness makes up in height for what it lacks in length." Abraham Lincoln says, "Most folks are about as happy as they make up their minds to be." The worst day that you can have is the day you have not laughed.

The optimist laughs to forget. The pessimist forgets to laugh. You might as well laugh at yourself once in awhile — everyone else does. The only medicine that needs no prescription, has no unpleasant taste and costs no money is laughter.

A smile is a curve that helps us see things straight. A smile is a curve that you throw at another and always results in a hit. A smile goes a long way, but you're the one that must start it on its journey. Your world will look brighter from behind a smile. So, smile often. Give your frown a rest.

Henry Ward Beecher said, "A person without a sense of humor is like a wagon without springs — jolted by every pebble on the road." Take to heart the words of Mosche

Wadocks: "A sense of humor can help you overlook the unattractive, tolerate the unpleasant, cope with the unexpected, and smile through the unbearable." Your day goes the way the corners of your mouth turn.

I believe that every time a man smiles, and even much more so when he laughs, he adds something to his life. Janet Layne said, "Of all the things you wear, your expression is the most important." Proverbs 17:22 reads, "A merry heart doeth good like a medicine." A good laugh is the best medicine, whether you are sick or not.

"The world is like a mirror; frown at it, and it frowns at you. Smile and it smiles too" (Herbert Samuel). Cheerfulness is contagious, but it seems like some folks have been vaccinated against the infection. The trouble with being a grouch is that you have to make new friends every month. Every man who expects to receive happiness is obligated to give happiness. You have no right to consume it without producing it.

The wheels of progress are not turned by cranks. Tom Walsh says, "Every minute your mouth is turned down you lose 60 seconds of happiness." Paul Bourge wrote, "Unhappiness indicates wrong thinking, just as ill health indicates a bad regime." It is almost impossible to smile on the outside without feeling better on the inside. If you can laugh at it, you can live with it.

It was only a sunny smile,
but it scattered the night.
Thus little it cost in giving,
it made the day worth living.

54

LOOKING
OUTWARD

NUGGET #21

THE GOLDEN RULE IS OF NO USE UNLESS YOU REALIZE THAT IT IS YOUR MOVE.
— DR. FRANK CRANE

A wonderful thing a person can do for his Heavenly Father is to be kind to His children. Serving others is one of life's most awesome privileges. Albert Schweitzer said, "The only ones among you who will really be happy are those who have sought and found how to serve." Pierre de Chartin commented, "The most satisfying thing in life is to have been able to give a large part of oneself to others." Proverbs declares, "He that despises his neighbor sinneth; but he who hath mercy on the poor, happy is he" (14:21). Follow the counsel of Carl Reilland: "In about the same degree as you are helpful you will be happy."

Hunt for the good points in people. Remember they have to do the same in your case. Then do something to help them. If you want to get ahead, be a bridge not a wall. Love others more than they deserve. Each human being presents us with an opportunity to serve. Everybody needs help from everybody.

John Andrew Holmes said, "The entire population of the universe, with one trifling exception, is composed of others." Too often we expect everyone else to practice the golden rule. The golden rule may be old, but it hasn't been used enough to show any signs of wear. We make a first class mistake if we treat others as a second class people.

You can't help others without helping yourself. Kindness is one of the most difficult things to give away since it usually comes back to you. The person who sows seeds of kindness enjoys a perpetual harvest. I agree with Henry Drummond when he said, "I wonder why it is that we are not kinder to each other... how much the world needs it! How easily it is done!"

Do you want to get along better with others? Be a little kinder than necessary. A good way to forget your own troubles is to help others out of theirs. When you share, you do not lessen, but increase your life.

Theodore Spear said, "You can never expect too much of yourself in the matter of giving yourself to others." The taller a bamboo grows, the lower it bends. Martin Luther King, Jr. said, "Everybody can be great... because anybody can serve." When you walk in the fruit of the Spirit others can taste of it. Harry Fosdick said, "One of the most amazing things ever said on earth is Jesus' statement, 'He that is greatest among you shall be your servant.' None have one chance in a billion of being thought of as really great a century after they're gone except those who have been servants of all."

Have you had a kindness shown?
Pass it on!
Twas not given for thee alone,
pass it on!
Let it travel down the years,
let it wipe another's tears,
till in heaven the deed appears
pass it on!

Henry Burton

58

A TRUE FRIEND IS
THE BEST POSSESSION.

Tell me who your friends are, and I will tell you who you are. The less you associate with some people, the more your life will improve. If you run with wolves you will learn how to howl. But, if you associate with eagles, you will learn how to soar to great heights. The simple but true fact of life is that you become like those with whom you closely associate — for the good and the bad. Almost all of our sorrows spring out of relationships with the wrong people. "Keep out of the suction caused by those who drift backwards" (E. K. Piper).

Any time you tolerate mediocrity in others it increases your mediocrity. We should pray: "Oh Lord, deliver me from people who talk of nothing but sickness and failure. Rather Lord, grant me the companionship of those who think success and will work for it." A true Bulgarian proverb confirms, "If you find yourself taking two steps forward and one step backwards, invariably it's because you have mixed associations in your life." If a loafer isn't a nuisance to you, it's a sign that you are somewhat of a loafer yourself. An important attribute in successful people is their impatience with negative thinking and negative acting people.

A true friend is one who is there to care. It's been said a good friend is like one mind in two bodies. Robert Lewis Stevenson said, "A friend is a present which you give yourself."

You'll find a real true friend remains a friend even when you don't deserve to have a friend. This friend will see you through when others think that you're through. The wisdom of Proverbs asserts, "Faithful are the wounds of a friend, but the kisses of an enemy are deceitful" (27:6). Choose your associates carefully. This old saying is true: "He that lies down with dogs, shall rise up with fleas." If you associate with those who are lame, you will learn how to limp.

Never become friends with someone because you both agree on negatives. Rather, find friends who agree with you on positives. "My best friend is the man who in wishing me well wishes it for my sake" (Aristotle). The Bible declares, "Iron sharpeneth man; so a man sharpeneth the countenance of his friend" (Proverbs 27:17). Thomas Carlyle observed, "Show me the man you honor, and I will know what kind of man you are, for it shows me what your ideal of manhood is, what kind of man you long to be."

If you were to list your greatest benefits, resources or strengths, you would find that money is one of the least important ones while some of your greatest resources are the people you know. My friend, Mike Murdock said, "Someone is always observing you who is capable of greatly blessing you." I believe that God likes to bless people through people. He has right associations for you in your life. A true friend sees beyond you to what you can be.

The way to make a true friend is to be one. Your wealth is where your friends are. Hold a true friend with both of your hands. Consider what Francesco Guicciardini said: "Since there is nothing so well worth having as friends, never lose a chance to make the right ones."

ADVERSITY HAS ADVANTAGES.

"Times of general calamity and confusion have ever been productive of the greatest minds. The purest ore is produced from the hottest furnace, and the brightest thunderbolt is the one elicited from the darkest storm" (Caleb Colton). The door to opportunity swings on the hinges of opposition. Problems are the price of progress. The obstacles of life are intended to make us better, not bitter.

Obstacles are merely a call to strengthen, not quit your resolve to achieve worthwhile goals. Bob Harrison says, "Between you and anything significant will be giants in your path." Oral Roberts reflects, "You cannot bring about renewal or change without confrontation." The truth is, if you like things easy, you will have difficulties. If you like problems, you will succeed.

If you have a dream without aggravations you don't really have a dream. Have the attitude of Louisa May Alcott: "I am not afraid of storms for I am learning how to sail my ship." Samuel Lover said, "Circumstances are the rulers of the weak; but they are the instruments of the wise." The Chinese have this proverb that says, "The gem cannot be polished without friction, nor man perfected without trials." It seems that great trials are the necessary preparation for greatness.

Roberts Liardon said, "For every obstacle you face, God has provided a scripture for your answer." Mike Murdock says, "If God 'cushioned' your every blow, you would never learn to grow." Instead, don't let your problems take the lead. You take the lead. The problem you face is simply an opportunity for you to do your best. It is a fact that conflict is good when you know how to move with God.

What attitude do we need to have toward difficulties? William Boetcker said, "The difficulties and struggles of today are but the best price we must pay for the accomplishment and victory of tomorrow." Lou Holtz advised, "Adversity is another way to measure the greatness of individuals. I never had a crisis that didn't make me stronger."

You will find that when you encounter obstacles you will discover things about yourself that you never really knew. Challenges make you stretch — they make you go beyond the norm. Martin Luther King, Jr. said, "The ultimate measure of man is not where he stands in moments of comfort and convenience, but where he stands at times of challenge and controversy." Turning an obstacle to your advantage is the first necessary step towards victory.

God promises a safe landing, but not a calm voyage. Life is as uncertain as a grapefruit's squirt. Consider what Sydney Harris said, "When I hear somebody say that 'Life is hard', I am always tempted to ask, 'Compared to what?'" We might as well face our problems. We can't run fast or far enough to get away from them all. Rather, we should have the attitude of Stan Musial, the famous Hall of Fame baseball player. Commenting on how to handle a spit ball, he said, "I'll just hit the dry side of the ball." Charles Kettering said, "No one would have crossed the ocean if he could of gotten off the ship in the storm." The breakfast of champions is not cereal, it's obstacles.

DON'T MEASURE YOUR SUCCESS BY WHAT OTHERS HAVE AND HAVEN'T DONE.

Several years ago I met with a friend whom I have known for over ten years. He looked at me and said, "John, I see all the great things that God has done in your life and how He has caused you to increase in every way. But, as I began to look at *your* life I became full of doubt as to what God was doing in *my* life." He said, "I saw what He had done in yours and I began to doubt that God was really working in mine because I had not had the same success that you have."

I turned, looked at him and said, "Well, if it's true that you feel bad because God has been good to me, then would it be true that you would feel better if I had had terrible failures and had been doing much worse over the past several years?" He gave me a quizzical look and he responded and said, "No, that would not be true."

I said, "Well, if it is true for one it is true for the other. Really, it shows how inaccurate your thinking is. What happens in my life has nothing to do with what God is doing in your life." Too many people know how to live everybody's life but their own.

You will find that God rarely uses people whose main concern is what others are thinking. I believe that Jesus saw judging others as a major waste of time. He saw that judgment halts progress. Judging others will always inhibit your forward motion.

Some are inclined to measure their achievement by what others have not done. Never measure your success by what others have or haven't done. You are either a thermometer or a thermostat. You either register someone else's temperature or your own. Pat Riley said, "Don't let other people tell you what you want." No one can build a personal destiny upon the faith or experience of another person. "Don't take anybody else's definition of success as your own" (Jacqueline Briskin).

Your faults will never vanish by calling attention to the faults of others. Many people have the mistaken idea that they can make themselves great by showing how small someone else is. It isn't necessary to blow out the other person's light to let your light shine. Instead of letting their own light shine, some people spend their time trying to put out the lights of others. What a waste!

If you think you are doing better than the average person, you're an average person. Why would you want to compare yourself with someone average? Too many people seem to know how to live everybody's life but their own. We need to stop comparing ourselves to others.

NUGGET #25

KEEP YOUR TEMPER.
NOBODY ELSE WANTS IT.

Don't fly into a rage unless you are prepared for a rough landing. Anger falls one letter short of danger. People constantly blowing fuses are generally left in the dark. If you lose your head, how can you expect to use it?

A Filipino saying advises: "Postpone today's anger until tomorrow." (Then apply this rule the next day and the next.) When you are upset, take a lesson from modern science: *always count down before blasting off.* Seneca quipped, "The best cure for anger is delay." Proverbs counsels, "He that is slow to anger is better than the mighty; and he that ruleth his spirit than he that taketh a city" (16:32 KJV). Blowing your stack always adds to the air pollution. You'll never get to the top if you keep blowing yours.

One of the worst fruits of anger is revenge. No passion of the human heart promises so much and pays so little as that of revenge. The longest odds in the world are those against getting even with someone.

Instead of revenge, consider what the Bible says: "Vengeance is mine, I will repay, sayeth the Lord. If thine enemy hungers, feed him; if he thirsts, give him drink; for in doing so thou shalt heap coals of fire on his head" (Romans 12:19b-20). Francis Bacon adds, "In taking a revenge a man is but even with his enemies; but in passing it over, he is superior."

Time spent in getting even is better used in trying to get ahead. Revenge is like biting a dog because the dog has bitten you. When trying to get even, you will always do odd things. "Vengeance is a dish that should be eaten cold" (An Old English Proverb).

Marcus Antonius reflected, "Consider how much more you often suffer from your anger and grief, than from those very things for which you are angry and grieved." David Hume said, "He is happy whose circumstances suit his temper; but he is more excellent who can suit his temper to any circumstances." Anger is a boomerang that will surely hit you harder than anyone or anything at which you throw it.

WHEN YOU MAKE YOUR MARK IN LIFE, YOU WILL ALWAYS ATTRACT ERASERS.

To succeed in life you must overcome the many efforts of others to pull you down. How you choose to respond to criticism is one of the most important decisions that you make.

The first and great commandment about critics is: *Don't let them scare you.* Charles Dodgson said, "If you limit your actions in life to things that nobody could possibly find fault with, you will not do much." Nothing significant has ever been accomplished without controversy, without criticism. When you allow other people's words to stop you, they will.

Christopher Morley said, "The truth is, a critic is like a gong at a railroad crossing, clanging loudly and vainly as the train goes by." Many great ideas have been lost because people who had them couldn't stand the criticism and gave up. A critic is simply someone who finds fault without a search warrant. One of the easiest things to find is fault. "The most insignificant people are those most apt to sneer at others. They are safe from reprisals, and have no hope of rising in their own esteem but by lowering their neighbors" (William Hazlitt). Critics not only expect the worst, but make the worst of what happens.

Dennis Wholey warned, "Expecting the world to treat you fairly because you are a good person is a little like expecting a bull not to attack you because you are a vegetarian." I agree with Fred Allen when he said, "If criticism had any real power to harm, the skunk would have been extinct by now." Remember this about a critic: a man who is always kicking seldom has a leg to stand on. Great minds discuss ideas, good minds discuss events, small minds discuss other people.

The Bible says to multiply, but too many critics prefer to divide. Don't allow yourself to become a critic. Jesus warns, "Judge not, that ye be not judged" (Matthew 7:1). You will always make a mountain out of a molehill when you throw dirt at other people. No mud can soil you except for the mud that you throw at others. The mud thrower never has clean hands.

You can't carve your way to success with cutting remarks. You will never move up if you are continually running someone down. I agree with Tillotson: "There is no readier way for a man to bring his own worth into question than by endeavoring to detract from the worth of other men." Henry Ford commented, "Men and automobiles are much alike. Some are right at home on an uphill pull; others run smoothly only going downgrade. When you hear one knocking all the time, it's a sure sign there is something wrong under the hood."

Remember this, if you are afraid of criticism, you will die doing nothing. If you want a place in the sun, you will have to expect some blisters and some sand kicked in your face. Criticism is a complement when you know what you're doing is right.

NUGGET #27

IF ENVY HAD A SHAPE IT WOULD BE A BOOMERANG.

Envy is the most ridiculous of ideas, for there is no single advantage to be gained from it. A famous old saying said "When you compare what you want with what you have, you will be unhappy. Instead, compare what you deserve with what you have and you'll discover happiness." It's not trying to keep up with the Jones' that causes so much trouble. It's trying to pass them. Washington Allston reflected, "The only competition worthy of a wise mind is within himself." Nothing gets you behind faster than trying to keep up with people who are already there.

If envy were a disease, everyone would be sick. Frances Bacon said, "Envy has no holidays. It has no rest." The envy that compares us to others is foolishness. "But they are only comparing themselves with each other, and measuring themselves by themselves. What foolishness!" (2 Corinthians 10:12b)

"Stop judging others, and you will not be judged" (Matthew 7:1). Envy is one of the most subtle forms of judging others. Richard Evans said, "May we never let the things we can't have or don't have, spoil our enjoyment of the things we do have and can have." What makes us discontented with our personal condition is the absurd belief that others are so much happier than we are. Thomas Fuller said,

"Comparison, more than reality, makes men happy or wretched."

Helen Keller says, "Instead of comparing our lot with those who are more fortunate than we are, we should compare it with the lot of the great majority of our fellow men. It then appears that we are among the privileged." Envy consumes nothing but its own heart. It is a kind of admiration for those whom you least want to praise.

An Irish proverb said, "You've got to do your own growing, no matter how tall your grandfather was." You'll find it's hard to be happier than others if you believe others to be happier than they are. Worry about what other people think of you, and you'll have more confidence in their opinion than you have in your own. Poor is the one whose pleasures depend on the permission and opinion of others.

St. Chrysoston reflected, "As a moth gnaws a garment, so doeth envy consume a man." Envy provides the mud that failure throws at success. There are many roads to an unsuccessful life, but envy is the shortest of them all.

HAVE...

Have peace enough to pass all understanding.

Have hope enough to keep your heart looking forward.

Have strength enough to battle obstacles and overcome them.

Have commitment enough to not give up too soon.

Have faith enough to please God.

Have fun enough to enjoy every aspect of life.

Have patience enough to let faith complete its work in you.

Have love enough to give to those who deserve it the least but need it the most.

Have focus enough to say no to many good ideas.

Have forgiveness enough to never let the sun go down on your wrath.

Have honesty enough to never have to remember what you said.

Have character enough to do in the light what you would do in the dark.

Have gratitude enough to say "thank you" for the small things.

Have purpose enough to know *why* not just *how*.

Have perseverance enough to run the entire race that is set out before you.

Have wisdom enough to fear God and obey Him.

Have responsibility enough to be the most dependable person you know.

Have confidence enough to know that you and God make a majority.

Have kindness enough to share what you have and who you are with others.

Have mercy enough to forgive and forget.

Have devotion enough to do the right things on a daily basis.

Have courage enough to face and fight any opposition to what you know is right.

Have optimism enough to know that God's plans are blessed.

Have trust enough to know that God will direct your steps.

Have expectancy enough to be on the lookout for miracles every day.

Have enthusiasm enough to show that God is in you.

Have obedience enough to do what is right without thinking twice.

Have direction enough to know when and where to go.

Have knowledge enough to have your mind continually renewed.

Have credibility enough to cause others to want to work together with you.

Have generosity enough to give before being asked.

Have compassion enough to be moved by the needs of others.

Have loyalty enough to be committed to others.

Have dependence enough to know that you need God.

NUGGET #29

EVEN POSTAGE STAMPS
BECOME USELESS WHEN THEY
GET STUCK ON THEMSELVES.

If you are only looking out for yourself, look out! Wesley Huber said, "There is nothing quite so dead as a self-centered man — a man who holds himself up as a self-made success, and measures himself by himself and is pleased with the result." Is your favorite letter "I"? Listen: "The core of sin is 'I' no matter how you spell it" (Ed Cole). The only reason pride lifts you up is to let you down.

Norman Vincent Peale observed, "The man who lives for himself is a failure. Even if he gains much wealth, power or position he is still a failure." Conceit makes us fools: "Do you see a man wise in his own eyes? There is more hope for a fool than for him" (Proverbs 26:12 NIV). The man who believes in nothing but himself lives in a very small world. The best way to be happy is to forget yourself and focus on other people. Henry Courtney said, "The bigger a man's head gets, the easier it is to fill his shoes." A swelled head always proves there is plenty of room for improvement.

"The greatest magnifying glasses in the world are a man's own eyes when they look upon his own person" (Alexander Pope). Egotism is the only disease where the patient feels well while making everyone else around him feel sick. Egotism blossoms but bears no fruit. Those who sing their own praises seldom receive an encore. Charles Elliot intones, "Don't think too much of yourself. Try to cultivate the habit of thinking of others; this will reward you. Selfishness always brings its own revenge."

While gazing upon selfish accomplishments, the arrogant often miss God by failing to see what He is doing. Rick Renner said, "Don't miss the plan of God by self-consumption."

When you are on a high horse, the best thing to do is to dismount at once. You can't push yourself forward by patting yourself on the back. Burton Hillis remarked, "It's fine to believe in ourselves, but we mustn't be too easily convinced." An egotist is his own best friend. The fellow who is deeply in love with himself should get a divorce.

Folks who boast of being self-made usually have a few parts missing. You can recognize a self-made man; his head is oversized and he has arms long enough to pat himself on the back. A conceited person never gets anywhere because he thinks he is already there. Change your favorite word from "I" to "You".

NUGGET #30

THE HEAVIEST THING A PERSON CAN CARRY IS A GRUDGE.

Forgiveness is the key to personal peace. Forgiveness releases action and creates freedom. We all need to say the right thing after doing the wrong thing. Lawrence Sterne said, "Only the brave know how to forgive... a coward never forgave; it is not in his nature." Josiah Bailey adds, "It is the truth that those who forgive most shall be most forgiven."

One of the secrets of a long and fruitful life is to forgive everybody, everything, every night, before you go to bed. Peter Von Winter said, "It is manlike to punish, but Godlike to forgive." When you have a huge chip on your shoulder, it causes you to lose your balance. If you would quit nursing a grudge, it would die. You don't need a doctor to tell you it's better to remove a grudge than to nurse it. Forgiveness is a funny thing. It warms the heart and cools the sting.

It is far better to forgive and forget than to hate and remember. Josh Billings says, "There is no revenge so complete as forgiveness." Richard Nixon said, "Those who hate you don't win unless you hate them, and then you destroy yourself." Unforgiveness blocks blessings, forgiveness releases blessings. Why aren't some prayers answered? Dwight L. Moody answered, "I firmly believe that a great many prayers are not answered because we are not willing to forgive someone."

Do you want to release the past and claim the future? Get a hold of what Paul Boese said, "Forgiveness does not change the past, but it does enlarge the future." Harry Fosdick said, "No one can be wrong with man and right with God." You can be wrong in the middle of being right when you don't forgive someone. "Protest long enough that you are right and you will be wrong" (Yiddish proverb).

The Bible says in Ephesians, "Let all bitterness, wrath, and anger, and clamor, and evil speaking, be put away from you with all malice; and be ye kind to one another, tenderhearted, forgiving one another, even as God for Christ's sake hath forgiven you" (4:31). Ask yourself this question, "If God is willing to forgive, then who am I to hold out?"

NUGGET #31

DO WHAT PEOPLE SAY CANNOT BE DONE.

Conservative talk radio show host, Rush Limbaugh, has a great name for his outlandish tie collection — *No Boundaries*. What a great slogan this makes for living our lives. We should do that which takes us out of our comfort zone. Be like David. Find a giant and slay it. Always pick an obstacle big enough to matter when you overcome it.

Until you give yourself to some great cause, you haven't really begun to fully live. Henry Miller commented, "The man who looks for security, even in the mind, is like a man who would chop off his limbs in order to have artificial ones which would never give him pain or trouble." Nothing significant is ever accomplished by a realistic person.

Tradition offers no hope for the present and makes no preparation for the future. Day by day, year by year, broaden your horizon. Russell Davenport remarked, "Progress in every age results only from the fact that there are some men and women who refuse to believe that what they knew to be right cannot be done."

Know the rules and then break some. Take the lid off. Melvin Evans said, "The men who build the future are those who know that greater things are yet to come, and that they themselves will help bring them about. Their minds are illumined by the blazing sun of hope. They never stop to doubt. They haven't time."

Be involved in something bigger than you. God has never had anyone qualified working for Him yet. "We are the wire, God is the current. Our only power is to let the current pass through it" (Carlo Carretto). Be a mind through which Christ thinks; a heart through which Christ loves; a voice through which Christ speaks; and a hand with which Christ helps.

If you really want to defend what you believe, live it. Dorothea Brand stated, "All that is necessary to break the spell of inertia and frustration is this: act as if it were impossible to fail." Do a right-about-face which turns you from failure to success. Keep this formula in mind: always act as if it's impossible to fail. One of the greatest pleasures you can find is doing what people say you cannot do.

NUGGET #32

THERE IS NO FUTURE IN THE PAST.

If you look back too much, you'll soon be heading that way. Mike Murdock said, "Stop looking at where you have been and start looking at where you can be." Your destiny and call in life is always forward, never backward. Katherine Mansfield advised, "Make it a rule of life never to regret and never to look back. Regret is an appalling waste of energy. You can't build on it. It's only good for wallowing in."

Consider the words of the Apostle Paul: "Forgetting those things which are behind and reaching forward to those things which are ahead. I press towards the goal for the prize of the upward call of God in Christ Jesus" (Philippians 3:13-14). You are more likely to make mistakes when you act only on past experiences. Rosy thoughts about the future can't exist when your mind is full of the blues about the past.

A farmer once said his mule was awfully backward about going forward — this is also true of many people today. Are you backward about going forward? Phillip Raskin said, "The man who wastes today lamenting yesterday will waste tomorrow lamenting today." Squash the "good old days" bug.

The past is always going to be the way it was. Stop trying to change it. Your future contains more happiness than any past you can remember. Believe that the best is yet to come.

Oscar Wilde said, "No man is rich enough to buy back his past." Consider what W. R. Ing said: "Events in the past may be roughly divided into those which probably never happened and those which do not matter." The more you look back, the less you will get ahead. Thomas Jefferson was right when he said, "I like the dreams of the future better than the history of the past." Many a "has-been" lives on the reputation of his reputation.

Hubert Humphrey mused, "The good old days were never that good, believe me. The good new days are today, and better days are coming tomorrow. Our greatest songs are still unsung." When depressed, you will find that it is because you are living in the past. What's a sure sign of stagnation in your life? When you dwell on the past at the expense of the future, you stop growing and start dying. Note Ecclesiastes 7:10, "Say not thou, what is the cause that the former days were better than these, for thou does not inquire wisely concerning this."

I agree with Laura Palmer's advice: "Don't waste today regretting yesterday instead of making a memory for tomorrow." David McNally said, "Your past cannot be changed, but you can change your tomorrow by your actions today." Never let yesterday use up too much of today. It's true what Satchel Paige said, "Don't look back. Something may be gaining on you."

"Living in the past is a dull and lonely business; looking back strains the neck muscles, causing you to bump into people not going your way" (Edna Ferber). The first rule for happiness is: avoid lengthy thinking on the past. Nothing is as far away as one hour ago." Charles Kettering added, "You can't have a better tomorrow if you are thinking about yesterday all the time." Your past doesn't equal your future.

NUGGET #33

THE JOURNEY OF 10,000 MILES BEGINS WITH A SINGLE PHONE CALL.
— "CONFUCIUS BELL"

Small steps...what a big idea! Dale Carnegie said, "Don't be afraid to give your best to what seemingly are small jobs. Every time you conquer one it makes you that much stronger. If you do the little jobs well, the big ones will tend to take care of themselves." Your future comes one hour at a time. Thomas Huxley observed, "The rung of a ladder was never meant to rest upon, but to enable a man to put his other foot higher."

Never be discouraged when you make progress, no matter how slow. Be only wary of standing still. A success is a person who does what they can, with what they have, where they are. Helen Keller said, "I long to accomplish a great and noble task but it is my chief duty to accomplish small tasks as if they were great and noble."

All glory comes from daring to take small steps. After being faithful in small steps, you'll look back and be able to say, "We're still not where we want to be, but we're not where we were." Julia Carney said, "Little drops of water, little grains of sand, make the mighty ocean and the pleasant land." Author Louis L'Amour wrote, "Victory is won not in miles but in inches. Win a little now, hold your ground and later win a lot more." God often gives us a little, in order to see what we will do with a lot.

"Nobody makes the greater mistake than he who did nothing because he could only do a little" (Edmond Burke). Small deeds done are better than great deeds planned. "Though thy beginning was small, yet thy later end should greatly increase" (Job 8:7). I believe that God cares just as much about the small things in your life as the big things. Why? Because He knows if you are faithful in the small things, the big things will take care of themselves.

The prize of doing one duty is the opportunity to do another. R. Smith said, "Most of the critical things in life, which become the starting points of human destiny, are little things." Do little things now and big things will come to you asking to be done.

One thing is for sure: what isn't tried won't work. The most important thing is to begin even though the first step is the hardest. I agree with Vince Lombardi: "Inches make champions." Take one small step right now. Don't ignore the small things. The kite flies because of its tail. It's the little things that count: sometimes a safety pin carries more responsibility than a bank president.

H. Storey remarked, "Have confidence that if you have done a *little* thing well, you could do a *bigger* thing well, too." Consider what Pat Robertson said: "Despise not the day of small beginnings because you can make all your mistakes anonymously." Value the little things. One day you may look back and realize they were the big things. Dante said, "From a little spark may burst a mighty flame." Remember this on your way up; the biggest dog was once a pup.

NUGGET #34

PROCRASTINATION IS THE FERTILIZER THAT MAKES DIFFICULTIES GROW.

Ask yourself: "If I don't take action now, what will this ultimately cost me?" When a procrastinator has finally made up his mind, the opportunity has always passed by. Edwin Markum said,

> When duty comes a knocking at your gate,
> welcome him in; for if you bid him wait,
> he will depart only to come once more
> and bring seven other duties to your door.

What you put off until tomorrow, you'll probably put off tomorrow, too. Success comes to the man who does today what others were thinking of doing tomorrow. The lazier a man is, the more he is going to do tomorrow. "All problems become smaller if you don't dodge them, but confront them. Touch a thistle timidly, and it pricks you; grasp it boldly, and its spines crumble" (William Halsey).

Wasting time wastes your life. Cervantes pondered, "By the street of By and By, one arrives at the house of never." A lazy person doesn't go through life — he's pushed through it. "The wise man does at once what the fool does finally" (Gracian). "Some day" is not a day of the week. Doing nothing is the most tiresome job in the world. When you won't start, your difficulties won't stop. Tackle any difficulty now — the longer you wait the bigger it grows. Procrastinators never have small problems because they always wait until their problems grow up.

In the game of life nothing is less important than the score at half time. "The tragedy of life is not that man loses, but that he almost wins" (Haywood Broun). Don't leave before the miracle happens! Robert Lewis Stevenson commented, "Saints are sinners who kept on going." The race is not always to the swift, but to those who keep on running. Some people wait so long the future is gone before they get there.

Most people who sit around waiting for their ship to come in often find it is hardship. Those things that come to a man who waits seldom turn out to be the things he's waited for. The hardest work in the world is that which should have been done yesterday. Hard work is usually an accumulation of easy things that should have been done last week.

Sir Josiah Stamp said, "It is easy to dodge our responsibilities, but we cannot dodge the consequences of dodging our responsibilities." William James reflected, "Nothing is so fatiguing as the eternal hanging on of an uncompleted task." People who delay action until all factors are perfect, do nothing. Jimmy Lyons said, "Tomorrow is the only day in the year that appeals to a lazy man."

The Bible promises no loaves to the loafer. "A man with nothing to do does far more strenuous 'labor' than any other form of work. But my greatest pity is for the man who dodges a job he knows he should do. He is a shirker, and boy! What punishment he takes....from himself" (E.R. Collcord). Carve out a future; don't just whittle away the time.

GO FROM . . .

Go from burnout to recharged.

Go from failure to learning.

Go from regrets of the past to dreams of the future.

Go from frustrated to focused.

Go from seeing God nowhere to seeing Him everywhere.

Go from prejudice to reconciliation.

Go from ordinary to extraordinary.

Go from defective to effective.

Go from despiteful to insightful.

Go from whining to winning.

Go from lukewarm to "on fire".

Go from security to opportunity.

Go from fear to faith.

Go from resisting to receiving.

Go from thinking of yourself to thinking of others.

Go from complaining to obtaining.

Go from drifting to steering.

Go from being a problem to being an answer.

Go from trying to committing.

Go from a copy to an original.

Go from envying others to serving others.

Go from ingratitude to thanksgiving.

Go from fault-finding to forgiveness.

Go from criticism to compliments.

Go from alibis to action.

Go from procrastination to progress.

Go from hesitation to obedience.

Go from blending in to standing out.

Go from fractured to focused.

Go from taking to giving.

Go from wishing to wisdom.

Go from the world to the Word.

Go from full of pride to full of God.

LOOKING
UPWARD

NUGGET #36

DON'T WAIT FOR ALL THE LIGHTS TO BE GREEN BEFORE YOU LEAVE THE HOUSE.
— JIM STOVALL

Don't do anything that doesn't require faith. G. C. Lichtenberg said, "Never undertake anything for which you wouldn't have the courage to ask the blessings of heaven." Ed Cole focusing on faith said, "There are three levels of knowledge. God is for me. God is with me. God is in me." Psalms 56:9 reads, "When I cry unto thee, then shall mine enemies turn back; this I know; for God is for me." Accept and acknowledge only those thoughts that contribute to your success, that line up with God's Word and His will for your life.

Wayne Gretsky is, arguably, the greatest hockey player in history. Asked about his secret for continuing to lead the national hockey league in goals year after year, Gretsky replied, "I skate to where the puck is going to be, not where it has been." Dare to go farther than you can see. "Seek not to understand that thou mayest believe, but believe that thou mayest understand" (Saint Augustine).

Too many people expect little from God, ask little, and therefore receive little and are content with little. Sherwood Eddie said, "Faith is not trying to believe something regardless of the evidence; faith is daring to do something regardless of the consequences." I sincerely believe that we would accomplish many more things if we did not so automatically view them as impossible.

God gave man an upright countenance to survey the heavens and look upward toward him. Don't ever say that conditions are not right. This will always limit God. If you wait for conditions to be exactly right, you will never obey God. The Bible says in Isaiah 1:19, "If you are willing and obedient, you will eat the good of the land."

Those who dare, do; those who dare not, do not. Isak Dineson said, "God made the world round so that we would never be able to see too far down the road." The person who dares for nothing need hope for nothing. You have reached stagnation when all you ever exercise is caution. Sometimes you must press ahead despite the pounding fear in your head that says, "Turn back."

If God is kept outside, something must be wrong inside. God will never allow anything to confront you that you and He together can't handle. Mary Lyon said, "Trust in God — and do something."

God said, "Come to the edge."
We said, "It's too high."
"Come to the edge."
We said, "We might fall."
"Come to the edge," God said.
And we came.
And he pushed us.
And we flew.

NUGGET #37

QUESTIONS

Do you put a question mark where God has put a period?

Do you tackle problems bigger than you?

Do you leave others better than you found them?

Is your favorite letter "I"?

In your prayers how often do you say, "And now, God, what can I do for You?"

Do you believe your doubts and doubt your beliefs?

And how does a man benefit if he gains the whole world and loses his soul in the process? (Jesus)

What would happen if you changed the words you spoke about your biggest problem? Your biggest opportunity?

Are you becoming ordinary?

Will people say this about your life: "He did nothing in particular and he did it very well"?

How much of you does God have?

Is it a long way from your words to your deeds?

If you try to be like him (or her), who will be like you?

Do you give up control of your life to something other than faith?

What kind of world would this be if everyone was just like you?

If you don't take action now, what will this ultimately cost you?

Are you a person who says "My decision is maybe — and that's final!"?

Are you making dust or eating dust? (Bill Grant)

Who of you by worrying can add a single hour to his life? (Jesus)

Do you count your blessings or think your blessings don't count?

Do you need a good swift kick in the seat of your "cant's"?

Are you known by the promises you don't keep?

Would the boy you were be proud of the man you are?

Are you already disappointed with the future?

How often do you ask God, "What are You up to today? Can I be a part of it?"

NUGGET #38

NEVER TAKE THE ADVICE OF YOUR FEARS.

Worry seems to be the sin that most people are not afraid to commit. We used to fear God. Now we fear everything else. Nicholas Berdyaev says, "Victory over fear is the first spiritual duty of man."

Fears, like babies, grow larger by nursing them. Fear wants to grow faster than teenagers. Disraeli says, "Nothing in life is more remarkable than the unnecessary anxiety which we endure, and generally create ourselves." We must act in spite of fear... not because of it. If you are afraid to step up to the plate, you will never hit a home run.

Sister Mary Tricky said, "Fear is faith that it won't work out." The Bible says in Psalms, "God is our refuge and strength, a very present help in trouble. Therefore we will not fear." Don't fear for the Lord is with you. He will never leave you to face your challenges alone.

Lucy Montgomery said, "It only seems as if you are doing something when you are worrying." Worry doesn't help tomorrow's troubles, but it does ruin today's happiness. "A day of worry is more exhausting than a day of work" (John Lubbock). When you worry about the future, there will soon be no future for you to worry about. No matter how much a person dreads the future, he usually wants to be around to see it. The truth is, more people worry about the future than prepare for it.

Never trouble trouble, until trouble troubles you. Arthur Roche said, "Worry is a thin stream of fear trickling through the mind. If encouraged, it cuts a channel into which all other thoughts are drained." Instead, do what Dr. Rob Gilbert advised, "It's all right to have butterflies in your stomach. Just get them to fly in formation."

Only your mind can produce fear. Jesus said, "Which of you by worrying can add one cubit to his stature?" We choose our joys and our fears long before we experience them. So I agree with Helen Keller: "It gives me a deep, comforting sense that things seen are temporal and things unseen are eternal." George Porter said, "Always be on guard against your imagination. How many lions it creates in our paths, and so easily! And we suffer so much if we do not turn a deaf ear to its tales and suggestions."

Worry never fixes anything. Shakespeare wrote, "Our doubts are traitors, and they make us lose what we oft might win, by fearing to attempt." Emanuel Celler says, "Don't roll up your pant legs before you get to the stream."

"If you are distressed by anything external, the pain is not due to the thing itself, but to your estimate of it and this you have the power to revoke at any moment" (Marcus Aurelius). Fears lie and make us not go where we might have won. There are always two voices sounding in our ears — the voice of fear and the voice of faith. One is the clamor of the senses. The other is the whispering of God. Never let your fears hold you back from pursuing your dream.

NUGGET #39

PRAY UNTIL YOU PRAY.

Amazing things start happening when we start praying. Prayer time is never wasted time. Charles Spurgeon taught, "Sometimes we think we are too busy to pray. That is a great mistake, for praying is a savings of time." A. J. Gordon added, "You can do more than pray after you have prayed, but you cannot do more than pray *until* you have prayed."

"The best prayers have often more groans than words" (John Bunyan). I experienced this when I had many pressing needs all around me. Honestly, I reached a point where I could hardly pray about my needs because they were so many. The only prayer I could manage was, *"Help!"* and I remember passionately praying it to God over 30 times until I experienced a breakthrough. Psalms declares, "O Lord, attend to my cry" (17:1). One of the smartest things I ever prayed was, "Help!" When you take one step toward God, God will take more steps towards you than you could ever count. He moved to meet my needs.

Prayer alone proves that you trust God. Oswald Chambers said, "We look upon prayer as a means of getting things for ourselves; the Bible idea of prayer is that we may get to know God Himself." Follow Dwight L. Moody's advice: "Spread out your petition before God and then say, 'Thy will, not mine, be done.' The sweetest lesson I have learned in God's school is to let the Lord choose for me." Do deep praying before you find yourself in a deep hole.

Prayers can't be answered until they are prayed. Nothing significant happens until you fervently pray; pray until you pray! F. B. Myer said, "The great tragedy of life is not *unanswered* prayer, but *unoffered* prayer." Byron Edwards said, "True prayer always receives what it asks for — or something better." God's answers are wiser than your answers. Ann Lewis said, "There are four ways God answers prayer: no, not yet; no, I love you too much; yes, I thought you'd never ask; yes, and here's more."

"Every time we pray our horizon is altered, our attitude to change is altered, not sometimes but every time. The amazing thing is that we don't pray more" (Oswald Chambers). Unfortunately, nothing is discussed more and practiced less than prayer. Pray with your eyes toward God, not towards your problems. Martin Luther said, "The less I pray, the harder it gets; the more I pray the better it goes." Frequent kneeling will keep you in good standing with God. Margaret Gibb said, "We must move from asking God to take care of the things that are breaking our hearts, to praying about the things that are breaking His heart." It is impossible to be prayerful and pessimistic at the same time. E. M. Bounds said, "Prayer is our most formidable weapon; the thing which makes all else we do efficient."

Mark Litteton said, "Turn your doubts to questions; turn your questions to prayers; turn your prayers to God." Prayer is not a gadget we use when nothing else works. Rather, I agree with O. Hallesby when he said, "Begin to realize more and more that prayer is the most important thing you do. You can use your time to no better advantage than to pray whenever you have an opportunity to do so, either alone or with others; while at work, while at rest, or while walking down the street. Anywhere!"

THERE IS SOMETHING FOR YOU TO START THAT IS ORDAINED FOR YOU TO FINISH.
— MYLES MONROE

Are you stumbling toward an uncertain future? You can predict your future by the awareness you have of your purpose. Too many people know what they are running from, but not what they are running to. First, concentrate on finding your purpose, then concentrate on fulfilling it. Having a powerful *why* will provide you with the necessary *how*. Purpose, not money, is your real asset.

When you base your life on principle, 99% of your decisions are already made. Purpose does what it must, talent does what it can. Considering an action? Listen to Marcus Aurelius: "Without a purpose nothing should be done." Robert Byrne said, "The purpose of life is a life of purpose."

"The height of your accomplishments will equal the depth of your convictions. Seek happiness for its own sake, and you will not find it; seek for purpose and happiness will follow as a shadow comes with the sunshine" (William Scolavino). As you reach for your destiny it will be like a magnet that pulls you, not like a brass ring that only goes around once. Destiny draws.

John Foster said, "It is a poor disgraceful thing not to be able to reply, with some degree of certainty, to the simple questions, 'What will you be? What will you do?'" Dr. Charles

Garfield added, "Peak performers are people who are committed to a compelling mission. It is very clear that they care deeply about what they do and their efforts, energies and enthusiasms are traceable back to that particular mission." You're not truly free until you've been made captive by your supreme mission in life.

Don't just pray that God will do this or that, rather pray that God will make His purpose known to you. William Cowper said, "The only true happiness comes from squandering ourselves for a purpose." Note Proverbs 19:21: "Whatever your plan is just know that nothing else will satisfy you." Know that God is with you and will provide what you need to accomplish your purpose.

Don't part company with your destiny. It is an anchor in the storm. A purposeless life is an early death. Psalms 138:8 reads, "The Lord will fulfill His purpose for me; thy steadfast love, O Lord endures forever." Rick Renner commented, "The only thing that will keep you from the will of God is if you look at yourself and say, 'I'm not so much among so many.'" You can't do anything about the length of your life, but you can do something about its width and depth. What you believe is the force that determines what you accomplish or fail to accomplish in life.

The average person's life consists of 20 years of having parents ask where he or she is going, 40 years of having a spouse ask the same question and at the end, the mourners wondering the same thing. Martin Luther King Jr. said, "If a man hasn't discovered something that he will die for, he isn't fit to live." Abandon yourself to destiny.

NUGGET #41

DO YOU COUNT YOUR BLESSINGS OR THINK YOUR BLESSINGS DON'T COUNT?

"If the only prayer you say in your whole life is "Thank you," that would suffice" (Miester Eckhart). Do you have an attitude of gratitude? If we stop to think more, we would stop to thank more. Of all the human feelings, gratitude has the shortest memory.

Cicero said, "A thankful heart is not only the greatest virtue, but the parent of all other virtues." The degree that you are thankful is a sure index of your spiritual health. Max Lucado wrote, "The devil doesn't have to steal anything from you, all he has to do is make you take it for granted." When you count all of your blessings, you will always show a profit.

Replace regret with gratitude. Be grateful for what you have, not regretful for what you have not. If you can't be thankful for what you have, be thankful for what you have escaped. Henry Ward Beecher said, "The unthankful… discovers no mercies; but the thankful heart…will find in every hour, some heavenly blessings." The more you complain the less you'll obtain.

"If we get everything we want, we will soon want nothing that we get" (Vernon Luchies). If you don't enjoy what you have, how could you be happier with more? Francis Schaeffer said, "The beginning of men's rebellion against God was, and is, the lack of a thankful heart." The seeds of discouragement will not grow in a thankful heart. Erich Fromm remarked, "Greed is a bottomless pit which exhausts the person in an endless effort to satisfy the need without ever reaching satisfaction."

Epicurus reflected, "Nothing is enough for the man to whom enough is too little." It's a sure sign of mediocrity to be moderate with our thanks. Don't find yourself so busy asking God for favors that you have no time to thank Him. I relate to what Joel Budd said: "I feel like I'm the one who wrote *Amazing Grace*."

"Happiness always looks small while you hold it in your hands, but let it go, and you learn at once how big and precious it is" (Maxim Gorky). I believe we should have the attitude of George Hubert, when he said, "Thou O Lord has given so much to me, give me one more thing — a grateful heart." The Bible says in Psalms, "Let us come before His presence with thanksgiving." Our thanks to God should always proceed our requests of Him. The Bible challenges us in 1 Thessalonians 5:17-18, "Pray without ceasing. In everything give thanks."

"We don't thank God for much He has given us. Our prayers are too often the beggar's prayer, the prayer that asks for something. We offer too few prayers of thanksgiving and of praise" (Robert Woods). Don't find yourself at the end of your life saying, "What a wonderful life I've had! I only wish I'd appreciated and realized it sooner."

Thank God for dirty dishes; they have a tale to tell.
While other folks go hungry, we're eating pretty well.
With home, and health, and happiness, we shouldn't
want to fuss;
for by this stack of evidence, God's very good to us.

BE...

Be...yourself.

Be...positive.

Be...thankful.

Be...decisive.

Be...merciful.

Be...persistent.

Be...honest.

Be...excellent.

Be...confident.

Be...prayerful.

Be...faithful.

Be...committed.

Be...dedicated.

Be...focused.

Be...forgiving.

Be...enthusiastic.

Be...hopeful.

Be...trustworthy.

Be...loyal.

Be...helpful.

Be...kind.

Be...happy.

Be...courageous.

Be...generous.

Be...loving.

Be...dependable.

Be...wise.

Be...holy.

Be...obedient.

Be...purposeful.

Be...effective.

Be...creative.

Be...responsible.

Be...devoted.

Be...patient.

Be...optimistic.

Be...compassionate.

NUGGET #43

WHAT YOU GIVE LIVES.

A good way to judge a man is by what he says. A better way is by what he does. The best way is by what he gives. Elizabeth Bibesco said, "Blessed are those who can give without remembering and take without forgetting." The big problem is not the haves and have nots — it's the give nots. The Lord loves a cheerful giver, and so does everyone else.

The secret to living is giving. Charles Spurgeon said, "Feel for others — in your wallet." An Indian proverb says, "Good people, like clouds, receive only to give away." In fact, the best generosity is that which is quick. When you give quick it is like giving twice. R. Browne says, "Whatever God does in your life is not so you can keep it to yourself. He wants you to give to others." When you give only after being asked you have waited too long.

The Bible says in Acts, "It is more blessed to give than to receive" (20:35). Giving is always the thermometer of our love. Eleanor Roosevelt said, "When you cease to make a contribution, you begin to die." Getters don't get happiness. Givers get it. When you live for another it's the best way to live for yourself. John Wesley advised, "Make all you can, save all you can, give all you can." That's a good formula for a successful life.

The Swiss say, "A greedy person and a pauper are practically one in the same." When it comes to giving, some people stop at nothing. Greed always diminishes what has been gained. Mike Murdock says, "Giving is proof that you have conquered greed."

A lot of people are willing to give God the credit, but not too many are willing to give Him the cash. Don't cheat the Lord and call it savings. The trouble with too many people who give until it hurts is that they are so sensitive to pain.

If you have, give. If you lack, give. G. D. Bordmen said, "The law of the harvest is to reap more than you sow." It is true: people who give always receive.

Henry Drummond said, "There is no happiness in having or in getting, but only in giving." The test of generosity is not necessarily how much you give but how much you have left. Henry Thoreau said, "If you give money, spend yourself with it." The secret to living is giving.

NUGGET #44

WHEN GOD IS ALL YOU HAVE, THEN HE IS ALL YOU NEED.

Billy Joe Daugherty said, "God is not hard to find! But there is a condition… we must seek Him with all our heart." You will always get into trouble when you try to handle your life without God. 2 Chronicles 32:8 reads: "With us is the Lord our God, to help us and to fight our battles." God, the ultimate warrior, lives in you. If you are a soldier for Christ, don't worry about public opinion. Only be concerned about your Commander's opinion. If you fear God there is no need to fear anything else.

I believe we should follow Mary Lyons advice: "Trust in God and do something." Satan doesn't care what we worship, as long as we don't worship God. Too many people ask the Lord to guide them and then they grab the steering wheel. Your relationship with God will last if He is first in your life. Too many people want God's blessing, but they don't want Him.

When you lose God, it is not God who is lost. Some people talk about finding God as if He could get lost. The Bible says, "Draw near to God, and He will draw near to you" (James 4:8). Tommy Barnett reflected, "The deeper I dig, the deeper He digs." To increase value, get to know God. Pray to God: "I want to be in your will, not in your way." William Law added, "Nothing has separated us from God, but our own will, or rather our own will is our separation from God."

Oswald Chambers advises us: "Get into the habit of dealing with God about everything. Unless in the first waking moment of the day you learn to fling the door wide back and let God in, you will work on a wrong level all day; but swing the door wide open and pray to your Father in secret, and every public thing will be stamped with the presence of God." Don't pray by heart, but with the heart.

The Bible finds us where we are, and with our permission will take us where we ought to go. Other books were given to us for information, but the Bible was given to us for transformation. A person who merely samples the Word of God never acquires much of taste for it. Psalm 35:27 declares, "God is always a plus factor. He is never a disadvantage to you. He is always an asset. He wants you to succeed and He has pleasure in the prosperity of His servant."

Our heartfelt cry to God ought to be the same as Isaiah's cry: "Here I am, send me" (Isaiah 6:8). Consider the words of W. H. Atken when he said, "Lord take my lips and speak through them; take my mind and think through it; take my heart and set it on fire." We must not only give what we have, we must also give what we are to God.

DO WHAT'S RIGHT, THE RIGHT WAY, AT THE RIGHT TIME.

Your success has little to do with speed, but much to do with timing and direction. What benefit is running if you're on the wrong road? The key is doing the right thing at the right time. Tryon Edwards said, "Have a time and place for everything, and do everything in its time and place, and you will not only accomplish more, but have far more leisure than those who are always hurrying." The problem is that many a go-getter never stops long enough to let opportunity catch up with him.

Beverly Sills says, "There are no shortcuts to any place worth going." The way to the top is neither swift nor easy. Nothing worthwhile ever happens in a hurry — so be patient. Because of impatience, we are driven out of God's will; continued impatience causes us not to return. Don't be impatient: remember, you can't warm your hands by burning your fingers. The less patience a person has the more he loses it.

God did not create hurry. Lord Chesterfield said, "Whoever is in a hurry shows that the thing he is about is too big for him." When you are outside of the right timing, you will sow hurry and reap frustration. There is simply more to life than increasing its speed. People that hurry through life get to the end of it quicker.

Brendon Francis commented, "Failure at a task may be the result of having tackled it at the wrong time." If the time has passed, preparation does no good. Leonardo says, "Time stays long enough for anyone who will use it." The trouble with life in the fast lane is that you get to the other end too soon. Soren Kierkegaard said, "Most men pursue pleasure with such breathless haste that they hurry past it." Haste makes waste: give time time. Many people overestimate what they can do in a year and underestimate what they can do in a lifetime.

Bruyere said, "There is no road too long to the man who advances deliberately and without undo haste; no honor is too distant to the man who prepares himself for them with patience." Many times the action that you take at the right time has no immediate relationship to the answer — it's to get you to the right place at the right time.

We are happiest when we discover that what we should be doing and what we are doing are the same things. You will never be what you ought to be until you are doing what you ought to be doing.

If you are facing the right direction, just keep on walking. Francis Bacon says, "The lame man who keeps the right road outstrips the runner who takes a wrong one... the more active and swift the latter is the further he will go astray."

Adopt the right pace: if you go too fast, you will catch up with misfortune. If you go too slow, misfortune will catch up with you. The Bible says, "Thy Word is a lamp unto my feet and a light unto my path" (Psalms 119:105). Let God be your guide and you will miss all the wrong places.

NUGGET #46

BE WHAT YOU ARE.

I have the opportunity to spend large segments of time in airports because I travel frequently. Almost invariably when in an airport, I notice scores of people who look like they are in a hurry to nowhere. Isn't it incredible that so many people devote their whole lives to fields of endeavor that have nothing to do with the gifts and talents that God has given them? Incredibly, many actually spend their entire lives trying to change the way God made them.

God knew what He was doing when He put specific gifts, talents and strengths inside of you. 1 Corinthians 7:7 asserts, "Each man has his own gift from God" (NIV). Marcus Aurelieus said, "Take full account of the excellencies which you possess and in gratitude remember how you would hanker after them if you had them not."

Robert Quillen reflected, "If you count all your assets you always show a profit." Seize the opportunities to use your gifts. "Put yourself on view. This always brings your talents to light" (Baltasar Gracian). Never judge yourself by your weaknesses. I agree with Malcolm Forbes who claimed: "Too many people overvalue what they are not and undervalue what they are." You are richer than you think you are.

Nathaniel Emmons said, "One principle reason why men are so often useless is that they neglect their own profession or calling and divide and shift their attention among a multitude of objects and pursuits." The best will always arise within you when you tap into the best gifts God has put in you. I agree with William Matthews when he said, "One well cultivated talent, deepened and enlarged, is worth 100 shallow faculties."

Too many people take only their wants into consideration, never their talents and abilities. Deep down inside, if you are a musician, then make music. If you are a teacher, teach. Be what you are and you will be at peace with yourself. I agree with William Boetecher who declared: "The more you learn what to do with yourself, and the more you do for others, the more you will learn to enjoy the abundant life." Do what's most natural for you. Yoruba said, "You can't stop a pig from wallowing in the mud."

I agree with Sydney Harris: "Ninety percent of the world's woe comes from people not knowing themselves, their abilities, their frailties and even their real virtues." Don't expect anything original from an echo. Musset said, "How glorious it is and also how painful — to be an exception." Billy Walder adds, "Trust your own instinct. Your mistakes might as well be your own, instead of someone else's." Abraham Lincoln mused, "Whatever you are, be a good one."

E.E. Cummings advised, "To be nobody but yourself — in a world which is doing its best, night and day, to make you everybody else — means to fight the hardest battle which any human being can fight and never stop fighting." The bottom line is — be yourself!

NUGGET #47

DON'T JUMP INTO
TROUBLE MOUTH FIRST.

Recently I saw a sign under a mounted large mouth bass. It read: "If I had kept my mouth shut I wouldn't be here." How true! What we say is important. Job 6:25 reminds us: "How forcible are right words." Let me pose this question for you: What would happen if you changed what you said about your biggest problem, your biggest opportunity?

Our prayer to God ought to be, "Oh Lord, please fill my mouth with worthwhile stuff, and nudge me when I've said enough." Proverbs 29:11 says, "A fool uttereth all his mind." Always speak less than you know. Never let your tongue say what your head must pay for later. The human tongue is only a few inches from the brain, but when you listen to some people talk, they seem miles apart. The tongue runs fastest when the brain is in neutral.

A high school track coach was having difficulty motivating his team to perform at its best. The team developed the distinct reputation of coming in last at every track meet they entered. One factor contributing to this less than successful program was the coach's pep talk tactics. His most effective inspiring tool, he thought, was to tell his team, "Keep turning left and hurry back." Your words have the power to start fires or quench passion.

Choose to speak positive, motivating, nice words. Pascal commented, "Kind words do not cost much. They never blister the tongue or lips. Mental trouble was never known to arise from such quarters. Though they do not cost much, yet they accomplish much. They bring out a good nature in others. They also produce their own image on a man's soul, and what a beautiful image it is." Colossians 4:6 counsels, "Let your speech be always with grace, seasoned with salt, that ye may know how ye ought to answer every man." Sir Wilfred Grenfell said, "Start some kind word on its travels. There is no telling where the good it may do will stop."

"The words 'I am' are potent words; be careful what you hitch them to. What you're claiming has a way of reaching back and claiming you" (A.L. Kietselman). Sometimes your biggest enemies and most trustworthy friends are the words you say to yourself. Henry Ward Beecher reflected, "A helping word to one in trouble is often like the switch on a railroad track... an inch between a wreck and smooth rolling prosperity." Johann Lavater said, "Never tell evil of a man if you do not know it for certain and if you know it for certain, then ask yourself, 'Why should I tell it?'"

The Bible says there is life and death in the power of the tongue (Proverbs 18:21). What words have the most powerful effect on you? George Burnham said, " 'I can't do it' never accomplished anything. 'I will try' has performed wonders."

If your lips would keep from slips;
five things observe with care;
to whom you speak, of whom you speak,
and how, and when, and where.

STAND FOR WHAT'S RIGHT. THEN YOU WIN, EVEN IF YOU LOSE.

The time is always right to do the right thing. "Be driven by excellence. To be driven by excellence that at the end of each day, each month, each year, and indeed at the end of life itself we must ask one important question: Have we demanded enough of ourselves, and by our example, inspired those around us to put forth their best effort and achieve their greatest potential?" (Richard Huseman) You achieve according to what you believe.

More harm has been done by weak persons than by wicked persons. The problems of this world have been caused by the weakness of goodness rather than by the strength of evil. The true measure of a person is in his height of ideals, the breadth of his sympathy, the depth of his convictions, and the length of his patience. Eddie Rickenbacker encouraged us to: "Think positively and masterfully, with confidence and faith, and life becomes more secure, more fraught with action, richer in achievement and experience."

"Of all the paths a man could strike onto, there is, at any given moment, a best path... a thing which, here and now, if it were of all things wisest for him to do... to find this path and walk in it, is the one thing needful for him" (Thomas Carlyle). The right train of thought will take you to a better station in life.

To try to do what's best and to remain essentially ourselves are really one and the same thing. Coach John Wooden said, "Success is peace of mind, which is a direct result of knowing you did your best to become the best that you are capable of being." One secret of success is being able to put your best foot forward without stepping on anybody's toes.

If you seek for greatness, then forget greatness and ask for God's will. You will find both. Harold Taylor said, "The roots of true achievement lie in the will to become the best that you can become." Elevate your personal standards of quality. Whatever you thought was good enough for now, add 10% more. Better is better.

The biggest mistake you can make in life is not to be true to the best you know. George Bernard Shaw remarked, "Keep yourself clean and bright; you are the window through which you must see the world." Follow Ralph Sockman's advice: "Give the best that you have to the highest you know — and do it now."

MIRACLES ALWAYS BEGIN IN THE HEART.

— BILLY JOE DAUGHTERY

When confronted with a new opportunity or tough situation, I usually ask myself, "Do I have a pure heart and a right spirit?" Psalm 139:23-24 prays, "Search me, O God, and know my heart; try me, and know my thoughts; and see if there be any wicked way in me, and lead me in the way everlasting."

The weapon of the brave resides in their heart. Horace Rutledge said, "When you look at the world in a narrow way, how mean it is! When you look at it selfishly, how selfish it is! But when you look at it in a broad, generous, friendly spirit, how wonderful you find it!" The Bible counsels us to prove all things, holding fast to those which are good (1 Thessalonians 5:21).

Margaret Mitchell spoke this truth: "There ain't nothing from the outside that can lick any of us." James Allen added, "You will become as small as your controlling desire; as great as your dominant aspiration." Remember this: when you don't have strength within, you won't have respect without.

If a person's aim in this world is right, he will miss fire in the next. Too many children are afraid of the dark, while too many adults are afraid of the light. William Hazlitt remarked, "If mankind would wish for what is right, they might of had it long ago." Roger Babson added, "If things are not going well with you, begin your effort at correcting the situation by carefully examining the service you are rendering and especially the spirit in which you are rendering it."

To know what is right and not do it, is as bad as doing wrong. Invite trouble and it will show up early. Save yourself a lot of trouble by not borrowing any. Here's more insight about trouble: you don't have to get rid of old problems to make room for new ones. Nothing costs more than doing the wrong thing.

The man who borrows trouble is always in debt. The best way to escape evil is to pursue good. The person who persists in courting trouble will soon be married to it. Go straight. Every crooked turn delays your arrival at success.

Pastor Joel Budd said, "A hungry heart is like a parachute. When you pull on it, it opens up and saves you." Keep your head and heart going in the right direction and you won't have to worry about your feet.

DON'T SIT BACK AND TAKE WHAT COMES. GO AFTER WHAT YOU WANT.

Let me ask you the age old question: "Are you waiting on God, or is He waiting on you?" I believe the vast majority of time, He is waiting on us. Is God your hope, or your excuse? I'm convinced He wants you to take the initiative, to live your life on the offensive. William Menninger said, "The amount of satisfaction you get from life depends largely on your own ingenuity, self-sufficiency, and resourcefulness. People who wait around for life to supply their satisfaction usually find boredom instead."

Albert Hubert remarked, "Parties who want milk should not seat themselves on a stool in the middle of the field and hope that the cow will back up to them." The door of opportunity won't open unless you push.

Being on the defensive has never produced ultimate victory. I believe that God helps the courageous. Do like Sara Teasdale said, "I make the most of all that comes and the least of all that goes."

E. M. Bounds said, "There is neither encouragement nor room in Bible religion for feeble desires, listless efforts, lazy attitudes; all must be strenuous, urgent, ardent. Flamed desires, impassioned, unwary insistence, delights Heaven. God would have His children encourageably in earnest and persistently bold in their efforts." When you are bold, His mighty powers will come to your aid.

Helen Keller said, "Never bend your head. Hold it high. Look the world straight in the eyes." If you want success you must seize your own opportunities as you go. I agree with Jonathan Winters: "I couldn't wait for success — so I went ahead without it." Lillian Hellman said, "It is best to act with confidence, no matter how little right you have to it." It is always a bumpy, uphill road that leads to heights of greatness.

George Adams said, "In this life we only get those things for which we hunt, for which we strive and for which we are willing to sacrifice." Don't just face opportunities and problems, attack them. Consider what B. C. Forbes said, "Mediocre men wait for opportunities to come to them. Strong, able, alert men go after opportunity."

NUGGET #51

ALPHABET FOR SUCCESS

A _____
Associations

B _____
Believe

C _____
Courage

D _____
Determination

E _____
Enduring

F _____
Forgiveness

G _____
God

H _____
Habits

I _____
Imagination

J _____
Judgment

K _____
Kindness

L _____
Laughter

M _____
Manners

N

Name (good)

O

Organization

P

Passion

Q

Quality

R

Reconciliation

S

Self-starter

T

Tenderhearted

U

Unswerving

V

Virtue

W

Worship

X

e(X)cellence

Y

Yes! Lord

Z

Zealousness

NUGGET #52

EXPECT SOMETHING FROM NOTHING.

"Faith is putting all your eggs in God's basket, then counting your blessings before they hatch" (Ramona Carol). And I might add, don't worry about Him dropping them. Faith is the force of a full life. I believe that the primary cause of unhappiness in the world today is a lack of faith.

Corrie Ten Boom says, "Faith is like a radar that sees through the fog the reality of things at a distance that a human eye cannot see." Faith sees the invisible, believes the incredible and receives the impossible. The Bible challenges us in 2 Corinthians 5:7 to walk by faith and not by sight.

So, what is faith? John Spaulding said, "Your faith is what you believe, not what you know." Dr. Alexis Carrel says, "It is faith, and not reason, which impels men to action… intelligence is content to point out the road, but never drives along it." I agree with Blaise Pascal: "Faith is a sounder guide than reason. Reason can only go so far, but faith has no limits."

Faith releases the miraculous. It is the way to God's divine influence. I agree with Pastor Tommy Barnett: "Faith is simply when you bring God into the picture." And, where do we meet God? "God meets us at the level we expect, not the level we hope" (Gordon Robinson). At times, faith is believing what you see isn't so. That's why the Bible says in Hebrews,

"Faith is the substance of things hoped for, the evidence of things not seen" (11:1).

Put faith to work when doubting would be easier. Faith is the anchor of the soul, the stimulus to action and the incentive to achievement. Faith will never abandon you, only you can abandon it. Nothing but faith can accurately guide your life. Faith gives us the courage to face the present with confidence and the future with expectancy. It is usually not so much the greatness of our troubles as the littleness of our faith which causes us to stop or complain.

Faith keeps the man who keeps the faith. No one can live in doubt when he has prayed in faith. Faith either moves mountains or it will tunnel through them. Saint Augustine said, "Faith is to believe what we do not see; and the reward of this faith is to see what we believe." J. F. Clarke said, "All the strength and force of man comes from his faith in things unseen. He who believes is strong; he who doubts is weak. Strong convictions precede great actions."

Faith is necessary to succeed. George Spaulding said, "Life without faith in something is too narrow of space in which to live." You'll feel cramped your whole life when you don't live by faith. As your faith grows you will find that you no longer need to have a sense of control. Things will flow as God wills and you will be able to flow with them to your great happiness and benefit. Colin Hightower said, "Faith is building on what you know is here, so you can reach what you know is there." Listen to Franklin Roosevelt: "The only limit to our realization of tomorrow will be our doubt of today." Let us move forward with strong and active faith.

A Final Word

Be the person God created you to be. Don't settle for anything less. Know this: "'For I know the plans I have for you,' declares the, Lord. 'plans to prosper you and not to harm you, plans to give you a hope and a future'" (Jeremiah 29:11).

Additional copies of
Conquering an Enemy Called Average
are available at fine bookstores
everywhere or directly from:

Insight International
P.O. Box 54996
Tulsa, OK 74155

Volume discounts available.

John Mason welcomes the opportunity to speak to your church, conference, retreat, or to men's, women's, and youth groups.

The following materials by John Mason are available from Insight International :

BOOKS:

An Enemy Called Average

You're Born an Original — Don't Die a Copy

Let Go of Whatever Makes You Stop

Words of Promise

Don't Wait for Your Ship to Come In — Swim Out to Meet It

Momentum Builders

Ask... (Life's Most Important Answers Are Found in Asking the Right Questions)

Conquering an Enemy Called Average

BOOKS-ON-TAPE:

"An Enemy Called Average"

"You're Born an Original — Don't Die a Copy"

"Let Go of Whatever Makes You Stop"

"Conquering an Enemy Called Average"

VIDEOS:

"Momentum: How To Get It, How To Have It, How To Keep It"

"Potential: There is Something Good Inside of You Waiting to Get Out"

ABOUT THE AUTHOR

John Mason, best selling author and speaker, is on a mission to attack mediocrity. He speaks to the gifts and callings in people's lives, drawing out their greatest potential. He illuminates purpose and direction in others and gives them the Word to launch out.

He is the best selling author of: *An Enemy Called Average*, *You're Born an Original —Don't Die a Copy*, and *Let Go of Whatever Makes You Stop*, which have sold over 500,000 copies. Each book is written and titled to fan the reader's potential into a blaze!

John is a popular and nationally recognized speaker at churches, conventions, and retreats.

Radio is also one of John's avenues for sharing this message. His captivating radio show called "Wait-A-Minute" is aired daily across the United States. This show is based on short excerpts from his books. Listeners have been changed by these bite-size truths for daily living.

Foremost, he is a remarkable husband and father. John, his wife Linda, and their four children: Michelle, Greg, Michael, and David reside in Tulsa, Oklahoma.